THE

OCTOBER

REVOLUTION

THE

OCTOBER

REVOLUTION

BEFORE

AND

AFTER

by E. H. Carr

VINTAGE BOOKS

A Division of Random House · New York

Preface

THE items which make up this volume were written at various times since 1950, the publication date of *Studies in Revolution*.

I is an expanded version of several lectures and broadcasts given in this country and in the United States in 1967 to mark the jubilee of the revolution of 1917: it has appeared in shorter forms in *The Listener*, 9 November 1967, and in *Revolutionary Russia*, edited by R. Pipes (Harvard University Press, 1968).

II was written as the preface to a translation of Chernyshevsky's *What is to be Done?* (Vintage Books, New York, 1964).

III is a conflation of two articles on Rosa Luxemburg published in *The Times Literary Supplement* in 1951 and 1966.

IV is a somewhat abbreviated version of the preface written for an English edition of Bukharin's and Preobrazhensky's *The ABC of Communism*, to be published shortly by Penguin Books in its series of Pelican Classics.

V is the slightly amended text of a BBC broadcast published in *The Listener*, 4 August 1955.

VI and VII were written as contributions to volumes of essays in honour of Herbert Marcuse (*The Critical Spirit*, Beacon Press, Boston, Mass., 1967) and of Maurice Dobb (*Socialism, Capitalism and Economic Growth*, Cambridge University Press, 1967).

VIII, IX (i), (ii) and (iii), and X are reviews published at various dates in *The Times Literary Supplement*.

I am indebted to Penguin Books for their generous agreement to the inclusion of the still unpublished preface to *The ABC of Communism*, and to the editors and publishers of the works and journals where the other items first appeared for their kind permission to reprint them here.

It will be noticed that the last three items were written as reviews of books by Isaac Deutscher, including his classic three-volume biography of Trotsky. The present volume of essays is, therefore, in a special sense dedicated to the memory of a friend from whose writings, conversations and criticisms over the space of twenty years I have learnt very much; I have included as a postscript to the volume a brief tribute which was published in the first issue of the *Cambridge Review* to appear after his tragic death in August 1967.

Trinity College, Cambridge   E. H. CARR
1 May 1968

Contents

THE

OCTOBER

REVOLUTION

I *The Russian Revolution: Its Place in History*

I SHALL interpret the term 'the Russian revolution' broadly. My concern is not so much with the ten days that shook the world in 1917 as with the world-shaking process of which they were the expression and sometimes the starting-point. Revolution automatically raises the familiar issue of continuity and change in history. It is a commonplace that no continuous situation, however static, is exempt from change, and that no change, however revolutionary, wholly breaks the continuity. But two observations are in point here. The first is that conservatives tend to dwell on the element of continuity – Tocqueville or Albert Sorel and the French revolution; in its extreme form, this attitude issues in the belief that revolutions have no fundamental significance, and represent merely the substitution of one ruling group or elite for another. Radicals, on the other hand, insist on the element of sudden and fundamental change – Engels and the leap from the kingdom of necessity into that of freedom, or Mao and the great leap forward. The second observation is that the elements of continuity in any revolution are in the nature of things those pertaining to a particular country, and the elements of wider or universal application are those of change. Since my interest on the present occasion is in the universal aspects of the Russian revolution, I shall emphasize the elements of change inherent in it, and not the elements of continuity which, in the context of Russian history, it undoubtedly displays. I shall not attempt to suggest that all the major changes which I wish to discuss were directly produced by the Russian revolution. Of these changes the revolution was in part cause, in part result, and in part symptom or symbol. All three intertwined relations constitute the 'significance' of the revolution of 1917, and help to explain its place in history.

The concept of revolution comes into modern history with the English revolution of the seventeenth century. For a thousand years, dissent, unrest, political and social change, had expressed themselves in religious terms. The English seventeenth-century revolution had marked religious overtones; the French revolution was the first purely secular revolution. But, when English writers called the events of 1688 'the glorious revolution', and then extended the term backwards to the still more dramatic events of forty years earlier, they were thinking primarily of the achievement of civil liberty, by which they meant a society based on the legally secured rights of individual citizens and not on monarchical authority, divinely or humanly ordained. In the turbulent middle years of the seventeenth century another idea had made a tentative appearance – the principle, broadly speaking, that one man is as good as another, and has the same rights as another – what we should now call the principle of 'social justice'. This idea seems to have flourished only in a few obscure and fanatical sects, and was safely smuggled out of sight in the glorious revolution. But it never entirely disappeared from the underworld of English history, and survived to become a dominant idea in all modern revolutions.

The French revolution, which stood before 1917 as the great prototype of revolution, was the first total and violent overthrow in modern times of a social and political order: this explains the immense impact it has made on modern history. It made this impact in three principal ways.

In the first place, the French revolution made liberty and equality essential rights of man and accepted goals of political action. The conception of the rights of the individual citizen was borrowed from the English revolution of 1688. English political theory and practice enjoyed an immense prestige among the intellectuals of eighteenth-century France. But the French revolution went beyond the rather simple ideas of political and civil liberty propounded in 1688. The idea of social justice, dimly adumbrated in seventeenth-century England, found more specific expression in the egalitarian ideology of the revolutionaries and, in particular, in the 'conspiracy' of Babeuf; and, though these demands were once more crushed when they took concrete form, the idea of equality could no longer be expunged from the revolutionary trinity. The French revolution had deeper social and economic roots than the English revolution, and more far-reaching economic and social consequences. In a phrase said to have been coined by Mirabeau and quoted by Napoleon: 'Ce n'est pas la liberté qui fait la révolution, c'est l'égalité.'[1]

Secondly, the French revolution – though this was no part of its original design – set its ideals in the future rather than in the past, and thus paved the way for a doctrine of progress. Theorists of the English revolution, true to the age-long habit of looking for authority in the past, had taken the view that what occurred in seventeenth-century England was not a process of innovation, but a reassertion of ancient liberties unjustifiably abrogated by the Stuart kings. The same argument was used a century later by the makers of what used to be called the American revolution; and no less a person than Tom Paine paradoxically attempted to defend the French revolution on precisely the same grounds: 'What we now behold may not improperly be called a "*counter-revolution*". Conquest and tyranny, at some earlier period, dispossessed man of his rights, and he is now recovering them.'[2] The myth of classical antiquity created by the Renaissance, and still immensely powerful in European eighteenth-century society, formed an anomalous strand in Jacobin thought and Jacobin oratory. The hopes and the enthusiasms kindled by the revolution superseded and replaced it.[3] Condorcet, more than any other single individual, marked the shift in the golden age of mankind from the past to the future.

[1] *Annales: Économies, Sociétés, Civilisations*, xiv (1959) 556.
[2] T. Paine, *Rights of Man*, Introduction to Part ii.
[3] This did not prevent it from retaining its hold on English and German education down to 1914.

Thirdly, the French revolution – here again through its consequences rather than by conscious intention – elevated the concept of productivity to a new and central place in human affairs.
In the hierarchical society of the *ancien régime*, the interest of
the rulers in economic affairs had been limited to the raising of
revenues from their subjects to meet military and administrative
needs. From the sixteenth to the eighteenth century, from Machiavelli through Colbert and his successors at the court of Louis XIV
to the Prussian cameralists, we can trace the line of slow development from the concept of the administration of the prince's
patrimony to that of the administration of the state; and this
development was marked by an increasing preoccupation with
efficiency in administration. But the ultimate end in view was to
meet the financial necessities of the government. It was left for
the Physiocrats and Adam Smith to insist that the wealth of
nations came not (as the mercantilists had taught) from trade, but
from production, to distinguish between outlay of wealth on
consumption and outlay on investment to promote further production, and to make the productivity of the whole society the
preoccupation of political economy. As Marc Bloch put it: 'Toute
la doctrine économique du XVIIIᵉ siècle – qui a légué ce tour
d'esprit à l'économie "classique" de l'âge suivant – a été dominée
par le souci de la production; et pour la plupart des économistes
français du XVIIIᵉ siècle production voulait dire avant tout
culture.'[1] The influx of wealth into new hands which preceded
the French revolution had its original source in trade. But, at the
moment when the French revolution was setting the scene for
the birth of bourgeois society, the industrial revolution in England
was rapidly expanding the sphere of economic activity and altering its character; in Marxist terms commercial capital was being
transformed into industrial capital. Here too, however, the revolutionary cult of liberty had its part to play. The sequel of the
French revolution and the industrial revolution was the rise to
positions of power and influence of a group of men whose earnings
from their individual economic activities provided the foundation

[1] *Annales d'Histoire Économique et Sociale* (1930) ii 333–4.

of the wealth and power of the state; and the main function of the state was to create and maintain the appropriate conditions of liberty for the untrammelled furtherance of these activities.

When Marx began to elaborate his system in the 1840s, he was the heir to all these revolutionary traditions. Liberty, expressed in Hegelian terms, meant the subordination of necessity to freedom, of blind economic forces to the conscious exercise of human reason; man was to be rescued from the self-alienation to which the existing social order subjected him, and re-instated as a 'social being'.[1] Equality found its embodiment in his idealization of a proletariat – the class which 'has a universal character because its sufferings are universal'.[2] Marx fortified the revolutionary faith in progress with faith in history as a meaningful process, and, by combining with it a belief in revolution as 'the locomotive of history', created the first theory of revolution. Finally, Marx stood on the shoulders of the Enlightenment thinkers and of the classical economists in treating production as the essential economic activity, to which all other categories were subsidiary:[3] and he was in essence right when he saw the key to the future in the hands of the industrial worker, and treated the individual peasant cultivator of the soil as an obsolescent unit of production. Marx regarded the mode of production as the constitutive element of society; the aim and essence of revolution was to change the mode of production. The *Communist Manifesto* proclaimed it as the aim of the victorious proletariat 'to increase the total of productive forces as rapidly as possible'; and one of the few glimpses afforded by Marx in his later writings of the communist Utopia was that here 'the springs of co-operative wealth flow more abundantly'.[4] Marx proved the most devastating of all the critics of western bourgeois society, precisely because he was a western thinker rooted in the presuppositions of bourgeois society, which he proceeded to carry to their logical conclusion.

[1] K. Marx, *Economic and Philosophical Manuscripts of 1844*, tr. Milligan (1959) 105.   [2] K. Marx, *Early Writings*, ed. Bottomore (1963) 58.   [3] Marx went further by treating production as *the* specifically human activity [K. Marx and F. Engels, *The German Ideology*, Engl. transl. (1965) 164].   [4] K. Marx, *Critique of the Gotha Programme* (Engl. transl., n.d.) 14.

Marx's vast synthesis of the French revolution and the industrial revolution embraced the future as well as the past. It was an unfinished revolution, both in the sense that its purposes had been fulfilled only in part, and required to be completed by further revolutionary action, and in the sense that their fulfilment would merely pave the way for further revolutionary aims to be achieved through another revolution. It was in both these senses that Marx once coined, or borrowed, the slogan 'permanent revolution'. It was appropriate that his name and doctrine should serve as the beacon for the next great revolution.

In the interval between the final elaboration of Marx's system and the next outbreak of revolution much had changed, but much also survived, so that, when we consider the historical significance of the Russian revolution, we see the interaction of a Marxist or pre-Marxist revolutionary tradition and a neo-Marxist or post-Marxist revolutionary environment. One thing which had not changed – or rather had been greatly intensified – was the emphasis on productivity. In the half-century before 1917 applied science was in process of creating a new technology of industrial production; mass production methods revolutionized the economics of industry; the production line and the conveyor belt created new problems of labour organization and discipline. The year 1870 demonstrated that the industrially advanced nation was also the militarily powerful nation; military power, as well as material prosperity, was a function of productivity. The Russian revolution for the first time explicitly proclaimed the goal of increased production, and identified it with socialism: Lenin's remark that socialism meant electrification plus the Soviets was a primitive formulation of this idea. It was repeated over and over again by Lenin and other Bolsheviks that the test of socialism was that it could organize production more efficiently than capitalism.[1] Modern Marxists have remained faithful to this doc-

[1] This did not prevent Lenin from recognizing that 'the victory of the workers is impossible without sacrifices, without a temporary worsening of their situation' (*Polnoe Sobranie Sochinenii*, 5th ed. xxxi 233). Bukharin provided a lengthy theoretical justification for the argument: 'In revolution the "husk" of productive relations, i.e. of the organization of human labour is "exploded"

trine, in theory as well as in practice. Among economists, as a distinguished American economist has remarked, 'the Marxists . . . have come closest to developing a substantial theory of economic growth'.[1]

The Russian revolution looked both backward and forward. It was the peculiarity of Russia's historical condition that she had both the need to catch up with western nineteenth-century achievements and the capacity to pass beyond them. Russia never really belonged to the nineteenth century; the great Russian nineteenth-century literature was a literature of protest not only against Tsarism, but against western bourgeois democracy and bourgeois capitalism. But at the same time the Russian revolution had to incorporate the achievements of the French revolution and of the industrial revolution and to recapitulate the material advances made in the nineteenth century by the west. This was expressed in Marxist terms by saying that the revolution of 1917 was the completion of Russia's bourgeois revolution as well as the inauguration of the socialist revolution. The campaign for industrialization started in the later 1920s aimed at the rapid transformation of the USSR into a modern industrial country – with military power and material prosperity as the twin objectives – through the application of the most advanced industrial technology; American aid and advice were freely sought and obtained in this process, since the United States was technologically the most advanced industrial nation, and hence the most deserving of imitation.

The success of this campaign, which in thirty years, starting from a semi-literate population of primitive peasants, raised the USSR to the position of the second industrial country in the world and the leader in some of the most advanced technological

---

which means, and must mean, a breakdown of the process of production and, consequently, a distinction of productive forces. If this is true – and it is unconditionally true – then it is clear *a priori* that the *proletarian* revolution is accompanied by an extremely steep decline in productive forces, since no revolution has experienced so far-reaching and so profound a break-up of old relations and their re-shaping on new lines.' [N. Bukharin, *Ekonomika Perokhodnogo Perioda* (1920) i 95–6.]

[1] E. Domar, *Essays in the Theory of Economic Growth* (1957) 17.

developments, is perhaps the most significant of all the achievements of the Russian revolution. Nor can the achievement be
measured purely in material terms. In the time span of half a
century, a population almost 60 per cent urban has replaced a
population more than 80 per cent peasant; a high standard of
general education has replaced near illiteracy; social services have
been built up; even in agriculture, which remains the stepchild –
or the problem child – of the economy, the tractor has replaced
the wooden plough as the characteristic instrument of cultivation.
It would be wrong to minimize or condone the sufferings and the
horrors inflicted on large sections of the Russian people in the
process of transformation. This was a historical tragedy, which
has not yet been outlived, or lived down. But it would be idle to
deny that the sum of human well-being and human opportunity
in Russia today is immeasurably greater than it was fifty years
ago. It is this achievement which has most impressed the rest of
the world, and has inspired in industrially undeveloped countries
the ambition to imitate it. This was the process foreshadowed by
Marx in the preface to *Capital*: 'The industrially more developed
country presents to the industrially less developed country a
picture of the latter's future.'

The world in which the USSR embarked on industrialization
was, however, a very different world from that of Marx. It was
not only technology that had advanced. Man's attitude to nature,
and his conception of his place in the economic process, had also
radically changed. The neo-Marxist world was a world of self-
consciousness.[1] The Russian revolution was the first great revolution in history to be deliberately planned and made. The English
revolution received its name *ex post facto* not from the politicians
who made it, but from the intellectuals who theorized about it.
The men who brought about the French revolution did not seek

---

[1] The terms 'self-consciousness' and 'consciousness', which are differentiated
in Hegel's *Phenomenology*, are used interchangeably by Marx and Engels.
Marx appears to prefer 'self-consciousness' in his earlier, more Hegelian,
writings, and 'consciousness' in his later writings, where he was concerned to
stress the subordination of 'consciousness' to 'being'; but the distinction is not
rigid.

to make a revolution; the Enlightenment was not in intention a revolutionary movement. The self-declared revolutionaries appeared only after the revolution had begun. The revolution of 1848 was a conscious imitation of the French revolution: this is presumably why Namier called it a 'revolution of the intellectuals'. But its one positive achievement was to extend to some parts of central Europe (where the peasantry was still a revolutionary force – which it had ceased to be in France, and had not yet become in Russia[1]) some of the results of the French revolution. The Russian revolution was also a revolution of intellectuals, but of intellectuals who not only repeated the past but planned the future, who sought not only to make a revolution, but to analyse and prepare the conditions in which it could be made. It is this element of self-consciousness which gives the Russian revolution its unique place in modern history.

The nature of the change is sometimes explained in terms of the differences between Marx and Lenin, of the transition from Marxism to Leninism. The problem is complicated by the evolution through which Marx himself passed. Marx down to and including the period of the *Communist Manifesto*, when revolution still seemed a live issue in France and Germany, was primarily concerned to propound a programme of action: the function of philosophers was not merely to interpret the world, but to change it. Marx, after he settled in London, was primarily concerned to analyse the objective laws of motion of capitalist society and to reveal the causes of its impending overthrow; political activities were the superstructure resting on the economic realities beneath. It was this mature Marxism – the Marxism of the *Critique of Political Economy* and of *Capital* – which, with its scientific and determinist emphasis, left its imprint on the rising European workers' movement in the latter part of the nineteenth century; and Leninism can be depicted as a return to the earlier Marx.[2] Nevertheless, though nearly everything

[1] On this point see G. Lichtheim, *Marxism* (1961) 363.

[2] Many of Marx's earlier writings which have received much attention in recent Marxist literature were first published in the 1920s and 1930s, and were unknown to Lenin as well as to earlier Marxists. Lenin's reputation as a

that Lenin wrote can be supported by quotations from Marx, the differences between them were profound and significant. The differences are sometimes explained as due to the transplantation of Marxism to Russian soil: Leninism is Marxism adapted to Russian needs and conditions. There is a grain of truth in this view. But it is more fruitful to think of the differences as the product of a difference in time: Leninism is Marxism of the epoch no longer of objective and inexorable economic laws, but of the conscious ordering of economic and social processes for desired ends.

The growth of consciousness begins in the economic sphere. So long as the individual producer and the small entrepreneur predominated, nobody seemed to control the economy as a whole, and the illusion of impersonal laws and processes was preserved. Marx's world-picture was firmly grounded in the past. He learned from Adam Smith that individual entrepreneurs and owners of capital were the essential agents of production in bourgeois society; and he followed Adam Smith and Hegel in believing that the activity of individuals, acting in their own interests, led in virtue of objective laws – the counterpart of the 'hidden hand' or the 'cunning of reason' – to results independent of their own will and purpose. Thus nobody consciously controlled the economic policies; and the product was master of the men who produced it. This was the realm not of freedom, but of necessity. The Marxist ideal, as Plekhanov put it, was 'the subordination of *necessity to freedom*, of blind *economic forces* to the power of human reason'.[1] Though Marx rejected the providential harmony of interests, he did, however, believe that ultimate harmony would result from the economically motivated action of individuals: this absolved him from any deliberate planning for the future. All economic thinkers from Adam Smith to Karl Marx believed in objective economic laws and in the validity of predictions derived from

philosopher has suffered the opposite mishap; it has been based mainly on the early and unsatisfactory *Materialism and Empirio-Criticism*, and not on his much subtler, though of course informal, *Philosophical Notebooks*, first published in 1929–30, and scarcely known in the west till a decade later.

[1] G. Plekhanov, *In Defence of Materialism*, tr. Rothstein (1947) 292.

them. This was the essence of 'classical economics'. The change
came when technological advance gave birth to large-scale capitalism. With the arrival of the mammoth manufacturing corporation and trading cartel, the economic scene was dominated by what,
in a masterly understatement, was described by economists as
'imperfect competition'. The notion of a self-regulating economy
in which decisions resulted from the uncontrolled interplay of
divergent interests was replaced by the notion of identifiable
people manipulating social forces to bring about a predetermined
objective. Economics had become instrumental – a matter not so
much of scientific prediction as of conscious regulation. Spontaneous price adjustment through the law of supply and demand
was replaced by price regulation for specific economic ends. It
was no longer possible to believe in a world governed by objective economic laws. The hidden hand that pulled the strings
was barely concealed by the velvet glove of the great corpora-
tions.

These developments made quite unrealistic the old conception
of the 'night-watchman' state, mounting guard to ensure fair
play between a host of small, independent, competitive producers.
Friedrich List, about the time when Marx began to think and
write, demonstrated the need for state intervention on grounds
of national efficiency in the organization of industry. Half a
century later in Russia, the first steps in large-scale industrialization undertaken by Witte owed nothing to individual initiative
and were an integral part of state policy. The socialists, though
they appear to have invented the term 'planning', were far
behind German industrialists, bankers and academic economists
in their recognition of the direction and the inevitability of the
processes at work. The first more or less fully planned national
economy in modern times was the German economy at the
height of the First World War, with the British and French
economies lagging not far behind. When the revolution proved
victorious in Russia, the case for planning rested both on socialist
precept and on the example of the German war economy. The
first long-term plan to be formally adopted in the USSR was the

plan of electrification in 1920. In the following years several industries, not excluding agriculture, prepared five-year plans, which were, however, at first regarded as rough estimates and not as mandatory prescriptions. The first 'five-year plan of the national economy' was adopted for the period 1928–29 to 1932–1933. Since then the USSR, except in the war period, has never been without its long-term plan; and five-year plans (or sometimes six- or seven-year plans) have proliferated round the world. If you wish to assess the historical significance of the Russian revolution in terms of the influence exercised by it, productivity, industrialization and planning are key-words.

The transition from economic *laissez-faire* to economic management by the state, from spontaneity to planning, from the unconscious to the conscious, had corresponding repercussions on social policy. The *Communist Manifesto* had accused the bourgeoisie of 'naked, shameless, direct, brutal exploitation' of the worker. Yet, so long as poverty or bad housing or unemployment could be attributed to the operation of objective economic laws, consciences were appeased by the argument that anything done to remedy these misfortunes would be done in defiance of economic laws, and would therefore in the long run only make things worse.[1] Once, however, everything that happened in the economy was seen as the result of a deliberate human decision, and therefore avoidable, the argument for positive action became irrefutable. Compassion for unavoidable suffering was replaced by indignation at unnecessary suffering. The concept of exploitation acquired a new dimension. For Marx exploitation was not an incidental abuse of which individuals were guilty, but an essential characteristic of the capitalist system, ineradicable so long as that system lasted. Exploitation now became a misdemeanour which could be prevented or mitigated by remedial action. A perceptive English writer in the first decade of the twentieth century diagnosed the change of climate, and defined by implication the

---

[1] In Great Britain this doctrine, as applied to the evil of unemployment, was preached by leading economists, financiers and politicians of all parties as recently as 1931.

character of the next revolution: 'The belief in the possibility
of social reform by conscious effort is the dominant current of the
European mind; it has superseded the belief in liberty as the one
panacea. . . . Its currency in the present is as significant and as
pregnant as the belief in the rights of man about the time of the
French revolution.'[1] The revolution of 1917 was the first revolution in history committed to establish social justice through
economic controls organized by political action.[2]

   The reassertion, due to the advance of technology and economic
organization, of the need for political action to direct and control
the economy, was reflected in a change of emphasis in Marxist
doctrine. Marx's nineteenth-century belief in the primacy of
economics over politics had been cautiously qualified, after his
death, by Engels's famous remarks about the mutual interaction
of structure and superstructure. The change fitted readily into
Russian conditions. At the turn of the century, the controversy
between the orthodox Russian Social-Democrats and the Economists, who wanted to give priority to the economic demands of
the workers, helped to shape and influence early Bolshevik thinking, and encouraged Lenin, in *What is to be Done?* and elsewhere,
to stress the primary need for political action. The Russian trade
unions were too feeble and too unreliable to play any role in
Bolshevik schemes of revolution. The Russian revolution was a
political revolution in an economically unripe country. Lenin, in a
remarkable *obiter dictum* of May 1918, observed that one half of
socialism – the political half – had been realized in Russia, the
other half – a planned economy – in Germany. Political action,
the dictatorship of the proletariat, was needed to promote an

---

[1] S. Leathes in *Cambridge Modern History* (1910) xii 15.
[2] Hannah Arendt stresses this aspect of the revolution from the standpoint of
a hostile critic: 'The whole record of past revolutions demonstrates beyond
doubt that every attempt to solve the social question with political means leads
into terror. . . . Nothing . . . could be more obsolete than to attempt to liberate
mankind from poverty by political means; nothing could be more futile and
more dangerous.' [*On Revolution* (1964) 108.] But does this say more than that
revolution, like war, which also leads to terror, is a bad thing, and that it is
better to solve social problems by peaceful means? The argument remains
inconclusive – except to total pacifists.

economic result, the building of a socialist economy. The assumption that, once the revolution had triumphed, the economic consequences would look after themselves was, however, falsified.
After the political episode of war communism, the introduction
of the New Economic Policy (NEP) in 1921 meant a partial
reinstatement of economic forces; and throughout the 1920s the
battle went on between the market principle as the guiding force
of the economy and the principle of planning. In theory everyone
accepted the assumption that it was preferable to achieve the
socialist goal through economic rather than through administrative action. In practice market forces proved unable to carry the
strain of intensive industrialization, and by 1929 had completely
broken down. The use of direct and conscious political means to
bring about economic ends has been since 1929 a persistent
leitmotiv of Soviet history, scarcely modified by the play-acting
of so-called 'market socialism'. Stalin in later years, in the short
history of the party published in 1938, and in his pronouncement
on linguistics in 1950, increasingly emphasized Engels's recognition of the role of the superstructure.

The dichotomy between economics and politics characteristic
of western nineteenth-century thought was reflected in the
familiar issue of society versus the state. When the Physiocrats
in France sought to free trade from the frustrating restrictions of
state power, when Adam Smith had his vision of a vast economic
process working independently of the state for the greatest benefit
of all, when Hegel set 'civil society'[1] over against the state and
made this dichotomy the foundation of his political theory, the
distinction between economics, which meant civil society, and
politics, which meant the state, was clearly established. Civil
society was the realm of economic man. Throughout the nineteenth century the argument proceeded about the desirable and
practicable relation between society and the state, but not about

---

[1] 'Bürgerliche Gesellschaft' should be translated 'civil society', not 'bourgeois society'; the term had not yet acquired its distinctive colour. Marx
defined it as 'the form of intercourse determined by the existing productive
forces . . . and in its turn determining these' (Marx and Engels, *The German
Ideology*, 47–8).

the reality of the distinction. In the English-speaking world, in particular, the opposition between society and the state, and the natural priority of society, became a fundamental category of political thinking. But Marx fully shared the same view: 'Only *political superstition* [he wrote in *The Holy Family*] today supposes that social life must be held together by the state, whereas in reality the state is held together by civil life.'[1]

In nineteenth-century Russia an embryonic bourgeois society was too weak to withstand the hypertrophy of state power; and after the revolution of 1917 a paradoxical situation developed. In western countries the persistence of the nineteenth-century liberal-democratic tradition continued to encourage a negative attitude towards the state, and an eagerness to denounce 'bureaucratic' abuses of its power, even while the constant encroachments of that power were recognized and accepted. In fascist countries the supremacy of the state over society was openly preached and practised. In the USSR the Marxist tradition also embodied a deep-seated hostility to the state, enshrined in Lenin's *State and Revolution* and in widespread denunciations of 'bureaucratism'. But this clashed with the Russian tradition of an absolute state power, and, in a period where the state was everywhere extending its functions and its authority, fought a losing battle. What is happening everywhere today is not so much the assertion of the primacy of the state, by way of reaction against the nineteenth-century assertion of the primacy of society, as a gradual obliteration of the distinction between them. The state becomes predominantly social and economic in character. Society identifies itself with the power of the state. The dividing line between economics and politics which was the essential feature of bourgeois society ceases to exist. These changes are strikingly illustrated by the way in which Soviet thought and practice has turned away from the Marxist attitude to the state.

Here we come to Lenin's most distinctive innovation in revolutionary theory and practice – the substitution of party for class as

[1] K. Marx and F. Engels, *The Holy Family* (Engl. transl. 1957) 163; both 'social' and 'civil' in this passage represent 'bürgerlich'.

the motive force of revolution. Lenin once again found himself in verbal agreement, at any rate with the earlier Marx. The *Communist Manifesto* foresaw 'the organization of the proletarians into a class, and consequently into a political party'; and Lenin, of course, constantly spoke of the class of which the party was the spearhead or vanguard. But the change of emphasis was marked, and corresponded to the shift from the world of objective economic laws to the world of political action designed to mould and modify the economy. A class was a loose economic group without clear definition or organization or programme. A party was a closely knit political organization defined by a common conscious purpose.

Both for Marx and for modern sociologists class remains an elusive concept. A class, for Marx, was an economic and social group bound together by a common relation to the means of production. It had no legal existence and no institutions. Its common action was the unconscious product of innumerable spontaneous actions of individuals pursuing their particular interests. This view of class fitted into *laissez-faire* conceptions of economic action and thought, and of the sharp dichotomy between society and state, which were dominant in the advanced countries throughout the nineteenth century, and was scarcely comprehensible in any other context. The embarrassments of attempting to apply the concept of class to earlier historical periods or to other continents are notorious. All authorities agree that the French revolution was a bourgeois revolution. This is not to say that it was started or led by an identifiable group or class answering to the name of the bourgeoisie; the class structure in France on the eve of the revolution was too complicated and mixed up for any such simplification. It is just as difficult to identify the bourgeoisie in pre-revolutionary French history as it is to attach any precise meaning to the term 'feudal', used by Marx as its class antithesis.[1] If, however, social revolution is defined as 'a social transformation in which the power of the obsolescent class is overthrown, and

---

[1] The term 'feudal' masks the fact that the nobility and the other 'orders' or 'estates' of pre-industrial society were legal categories and plainly not classes in the Marxist sense; but a feudal class is still more puzzling.

that of the progressive, revolutionary class is established in its place',[1] the credentials of the French revolution as a bourgeois revolution are fully vindicated. It was a bourgeois revolution not in the sense that it was made by the bourgeoisie, but in the sense that it substituted for the hierarchical society of the *ancien régime* a new type of society dominated by the bourgeoisie. To speak of a class struggle in France in the context of the French revolution is to anticipate the consequences of the revolution, not to describe its antecedents. 'Pre-industrial society', it has been well remarked, '. . . did not invest the concept of class with an operational meaning.'[2] It was only after the revolution that class became a useful cutting-tool of analysis, and was wielded as such by Marx with incomparable power.

The only class which really comes to life in Marx's writings is the bourgeoisie; nearly everything written by him about class in general relates, consciously or unconsciously, to the bourgeoisie in particular.[3] The unplanned and unconscious common action of innumerable individuals determined the policies of bourgeois governments, and constituted 'the dictatorship of the bourgeoisie'. The proletariat as a class was envisaged by Marx on the same model. Increasingly intolerable economic conditions would drive the workers to take action in defence of their interests. The workers of the world would spontaneously unite; and this common action would bring about the overthrow of the bourgeoisie and the dictatorship of the proletariat. Marx made it clear that this did not imply consciously planned action: 'The question is not what this or that proletarian, or even the whole proletariat at the moment, *considers* as its aim. The question is, *what the proletariat is*, and what, consequent on that *being*, it will be compelled to do.'[4]

---

[1] *Grundlagen der Marxistischen Philosophie*, German transl. (Berlin 1953) 551; this is the current official textbook.   [2] Lichtheim, *Marxism*, 381.
[3] As Wetter says [*Soviet Ideology Today* (1966) 203], Marx's well-known aphorism, 'The hand-mill gives you society with the feudal lord; the steam-mill society with the industrial capitalist', has meaning only as a statement about industrial society, not as a statement about feudal society. The hand-mill was not peculiar to feudal society, and is introduced here merely to point a contrast with capitalism.   [4] Marx and Engels, *The Holy Family*, 53.

Marx knew well that only a small proportion of the proletariat was as yet class-conscious (though, living in England, he may have tended to exaggerate this proportion); and he recognized the existence of a *Lumpenproletariat*, an unorganized and unreliable mass of low-grade workers. At the other end of the scale, Engels noted the birth in England of what he called 'a bourgeois working class', of a stratum of workers who showed signs of making common cause with the capitalists. But Marxists as a whole were not troubled by these threats to the international solidarity of the proletariat. It was assumed that time would correct these anomalies, and that at the right moment the workers would play their historical role, like the bourgeoisie before them, as a unified class. The contradictions of the capitalist system, and the pressures engendered by it, would sap its progressive and expansive capacities, and provoke a revolt by an increasingly numerous and increasingly impoverished proletariat. This would be the last revolution, which would overthrow the last ruling class, the bourgeoisie, and usher in the classless society.

When Lenin surveyed the scene – and the Russian scene in particular – at the turn of the century, the prospect was obscure. In the countries of the Second International, while few signs had appeared of an imminent proletarian revolution, the organization of the workers had made giant strides; and everyone appeared to agree that this was an encouraging token of their growing solidarity and revolutionary potential. In Russia workers' organization was primitive, and revolutionary hopes seemed infinitely remote. In *What is to be Done?* Lenin wrote: 'The spontaneous struggle of the proletariat will not become a genuine "class struggle" until it is led by a strong organization of revolutionaries.'[1] Logically Lenin set to work to create a party to galvanize the Russian workers into action; and in Russian conditions the work of a party on Russian soil was necessarily secret and conspiratorial. These preparations seemed in no sense a departure from the Marxist tradition or from the models created by the great Social-Democratic parties of the west; they were merely

[1] Lenin, *Polnoe Sobranie Sochinenii*, 5th ed. vi 135.

another desperate Russian attempt to 'catch up' with the west. What was bewildering and decisive was what happened in 1914 and 1917 – the negative and positive sides of the same medal. The outbreak of war in 1914 struck a crucial and long-awaited blow at the nineteenth-century capitalist system, and found the workers of the advanced countries rallying to its defence in their respective national uniforms; the traumatic effect on Lenin of this incredible experience is well known. The revolution of 1917 put in power the first government professing allegiance to Marxism and dedicated to the overthrow of capitalism; and this occurred in an economically backward country with a small, undeveloped and relatively unorganized proletariat. This reversal of the expected order of events confronted the Bolsheviks with the task of maintaining and defending the victorious Russian revolution in a hostile environment with woefully inadequate resources, human and material, at their disposal.

This crisis evoked a response already familiar in Russian revolutionary history. For the best part of a century, the Russian intelligentsia – a group without precise counterpart elsewhere – had provided the leadership and the inspiration for a series of revolutionary movements. When Lenin, in *What is to be Done?*, published in 1902, pleaded for a party of professional revolutionaries under intellectual leadership to spearhead the proletarian revolution, Trotsky contemptuously observed that the Marxist beliefs of intellectuals were 'no substitute for a politically developed proletariat', and accused the Bolshevik Party of attempting 'to *substitute* itself for the working class'.[1] When, however, the survival of the revolutionary regime was placed in jeopardy by the inadequacy, quantitative and qualitative, of the proletariat, the party, led and organized mainly by intellectuals, stepped into the gap. The Russian revolution was made and saved not by a

---

[1] N. Trotsky, *Nashi Politicheskie Zadachi* (Geneva, 1904) 23, 50 and *passim*. Later Trotsky evidently became more reconciled to the idea; in an article of 1908 (*Sochineniya*, xx 327–42), he described the Decembrists of 1825 as substituting themselves for a not yet existing bourgeoisie. He did not cite the intellectual leaders of the narodnik movement, whose 'going to the people' campaign in the 1870s enjoyed little success.

class, but by a party proclaiming itself to be the representative
and vanguard of a class. It was a solution consonant with the
Russian revolutionary tradition. But, more important, it was a
solution which marked the distance travelled since the days of
Marx. That Leninism was not exclusively or primarily a product
of Russian conditions is suggested by the fact that the two
major Marxist theorists after Lenin, who further elaborated the
Leninist notion of creative vanguards, were both non-Russians:
Lukacs and Gramsci. The Leninist gloss on Marxism belonged to
an age which thought of effective force as the product, no longer of
the spontaneous action of a mass of individuals, but of conscious
political planning.

The *Communist Manifesto* recognized the role of leadership
exercised by communists as the only fully class-conscious members
of the proletariat and of proletarian parties. But it was a condition of the proletarian revolution that communist consciousness
should spread to a majority of the workers. Marx attributed to
Blanqui, and rejected as heretical, a belief in the revolutionary
seizure of power by a disciplined minority. But for Marx consciousness was still primarily consciousness of a process which
remained outside conscious control. Lenin's conception of the
party as the vanguard of the class contained elitist elements
absent from Marx's writings, and was the product of a period
when political writers were turning their attention more and
more to the problem of elites. The party was to lead and inspire
the mass of workers; its own membership was to remain small
and select. In the months between February and October 1917,
it was a favourite Menshevik taunt that Lenin was a disciple of
Blanqui or Bakunin, not of Marx. On the eve of the February
revolution of 1917 the Bolsheviks appear to have numbered no
more than 23,000; and, though members flowed in between
February and October, the party in whose name the revolution
was made and governmental power assumed probably did not
much exceed 100,000.[1] But it would be an error to suppose that

[1] Official party statistics put the membership at 23,000 in January 1917 and
115,000 in January 1918 (*Bol'shaya Sovetskaya Entsiklopediya*, 1st ed. (1930)

Lenin regarded the revolution as the work of a minority. His fullest account of what created a revolutionary situation was given in the pamphlet *The Infantile Disease of 'Leftism'* which he prepared for the Second Congress of the Communist International in 1920. 'Only when *"the lower layers* (nizy)" *are not willing* to put up with the old, and "the top layers (verkhi)" *are not able to go on in the old way*, only then can the revolution triumph. In other words, this truth can be expressed as follows: revolution is impossible without a general national crisis affecting both exploited and exploiters.'[1] The task of leading the masses was not, properly understood, a task of indoctrination, of creating a consciousness that was not there, but of evoking a latent consciousness; and this latent consciousness of the masses was an essential condition of revolution. Lenin, within the circle of party leaders, was capable of taking up the position of a dictator. But he never did so in relation to the masses of the workers; and to this he owed much of his immense hold over them. His profession of willingness to learn from the masses was never an empty pretence. Lenin emphatically did not believe in revolution from above. Already in April 1917 he had written: 'The commune, i.e. the Soviets, does not "introduce", does not propose to "introduce", and must not "introduce", any transformations which have not matured both absolutely and in economic reality, and in the consciousness of the overwhelming majority of the people.'[2] And a year later, at the party congress which approved the ratification of the Brest-Litovsk treaty, he repeated still more emphatically: 'Socialism cannot be introduced by a minority – the party. It can be introduced only by tens of millions when they learn to do it themselves.'[3]

Some critics have found an element of political casuistry in this attempt to combine an elite leadership with mass consciousness. The embarrassed and sometimes contradictory utterances of the

---

xi 531); much larger estimates quoted elsewhere look like exaggerations made either at the time to encourage optimism, or *ex post facto* to refute the impression that the revolution was the work of an insignificant minority.

[1] Lenin, *Polnoe Sobranie Sochinenii*, 5th ed. xli 69–70.
[2] Ibid. xxxi 163–4.   [3] Ibid. xxxvi 53.

Bolshevik leaders about class contrast with their precise and rigid conceptions of party. After Lenin's death, sinister developments occurred, the seeds of which had undoubtedly been sown in Lenin's lifetime. Before the revolution some attention had been paid to the growth, in western political parties, of central party organizations and party bureaucracies which effectively determined party policy, and controlled the rank and file of party members.[1] In the Russian Social-Democratic Party tension had existed from the first between divergent conceptions of the party as a mass organization and as a vanguard leading and instructing the masses. After the revolution, the problems of survival and material progress confronting a revolutionary regime isolated in a hostile world were so vast and so pressing that Lenin's successors lacked the capacity or the patience to evoke that measure of mass consciousness and mass support which Lenin had had behind him in the period of the revolution and the civil war, and took the short cut – always the temptation that lies in wait for an elite – of imposing their will, by measures of increasingly naked force, on the mass of the population and on the mass of the party. Stalin's once famous short history of the Communist Party called the collectivization of agriculture 'a revolution from above, on the initiative of state power, with direct support from below'; and, though the phrase 'revolution from above' has since been condemned as heretical, it was symptomatic of the Stalinist epoch.

These developments were due in part to the peculiarly exacting nature of the problems which the revolutionary regime in Russia had to face, and in part to the peculiar conditions of a country where primitive peasants formed more than 80 per cent of the population, and the number of trained and politically conscious workers, comparable to the organized workers of the west, was infinitesimally small. But they were also, and more significantly, a product of the period. The French revolutionary slogan of equality was a necessary and effective protest against privilege in a highly stratified society. For Marx this problem, like every

---

[1] The classical works of Ostrogorski and R. Michels are frequently quoted in this context.

social problem, was a problem of the relations of production. Capitalist society was based on the exploitation of man by man; the principle of inequality was built into the capitalist division of labour. In a famous passage of *Capital*, Marx reiterated the belief, common to many nineteenth-century writers, that large-scale industry would 'make an end of the manufacturing division of labour in which each man is tied for life to a single detail operation'.[1] The Marxist Utopia contemplated the breaking down of the differentiation between different forms of labour – notably between manual and intellectual work. Lenin's *State and Revolution*, with its vision of the work of administration performed by ordinary workers in rotation, and the initial experiments of the Bolshevik revolution in workers' control in the factories, were the last belated tributes to this conception.

The vision quickly faded, and the experiments ended in failure. Marx himself, in a later chapter of *Capital* which appeared posthumously in the third volume, took a more realistic view of the future of labour:

> Freedom in this field can only consist in socialised man, the associated producers, rationally regulating their interchange with nature, bringing it under their common control, instead of being ruled by it as the blind forces of nature. . . . But it nonetheless still remains a realm of necessity. Beyond it begins that development of human energy which is an end in itself, the true realm of freedom, which can, however, only blossom forth with this realm of necessity as its basis.[2]

Lenin, as early as March 1918, came out in support of what was later called 'one-man management' (edinonachalie) in factories in terms so emphatic that the passage has sometimes been unfairly quoted out of context as a defence of political dictatorship.[3] The problem is not confined to the degree of discipline required to

[1] K. Marx, *Capital*, 1 (transl. Moore and Aveling 1954) 522.

[2] Marx, *Capital*, 3 (Engl. transl. 1960) 800. In his note-books Marx remarked that 'labour cannot become play, as Fourier wants to make it' [*Grundrisse der Kritik der Politischen Ökonomie* (1953) 599]; contrast this with Engels's naïve optimism: 'Productive labour will become a pleasure instead of a burden.' [*Anti-Dühring* (Engl. transl. 1954) 408.]

[3] Lenin, *Polnoe Sobranie Sochinenii*, 5th ed. xxxvi 200.

enforce performance of a necessary minimum of arduous and repellent physical labour. It is correct that both the scope and the harsh character of such labour has diminished over the past century, though its total elimination still seems a utopian dream. But the bold nineteenth-century assumption that technological progress would reduce the need of specialization and thus obliterate distinctions between different forms of labour, and especially between intellectual and manual labour, has been signally falsified. A new kind of stratification has entered into every branch of administration and production. The need for technological and administrative elites declares itself at every level – in government, in industrial organization, on the factory floor and on the farm – and is likely to increase with the increasing complexity of administrative and productive processes.

When, therefore, Stalin shocked the world in June 1931 by denouncing egalitarianism or 'levelling' (*uravnilovka*), and remarked that 'every industry, every enterprise, every workshop' had its 'leading groups', and later accused supporters of egalitarianism of 'petty-bourgeois views',[1] he struck a shrewder blow than was realized by his critics at the time. The ideal of equality launched by the French revolution found increasingly widespread acceptance and application in the western world of the nineteenth century; before the end of the century, the need to extend it from the political to the economic sphere had begun to be recognized. Since 1917 dramatic strides have been made, in the Soviet Union and in other countries, towards improving the standards of living of the industrial worker. But this process has been accompanied by an insidious spread of elitist doctrines, avowed or disguised, and by a growing recognition of the difficulty of reconciling the need for administrative and technological elites with the egalitarian aspirations which mass democracy inherited from the French revolution.[2] The fact that many of these elites would call themselves non-political does not mean that they do

[1] J. Stalin, *Sochineniya*, xiii 58–60, 357.
[2] For a further discussion of the contemporary problem of equality see pp. 77–9 below.

not wield decisive political influence. 'Bureaucracy' and 'technocracy' are not empty words. The autocrats of the past have been replaced by anonymous Kafka-like figures, whom we cannot control and often cannot identify. The need, with which Lenin wrestled and which Stalin contemptuously dismissed, of reconciling elite leadership with mass democracy has emerged as a key problem in the Soviet Union today. Nor is the problem, though spotlighted by the sequel of the Bolshevik revolution, of exclusive significance to a single country. It would be rash to dismiss the Russian experience as irrelevant to our own, or to be unduly complacent about our own solutions. It would be rasher still to think of it as irrelevant to the problems of countries all over the world which have no experience of an established democracy in the past.

The educational function of the elite was strongly emphasized by Lenin in *What is to be Done?* Marx, like Adam Smith and Hegel, believed that individuals conformed to, and were the agents or victims of, objective social and economic laws of which they were, nevertheless, unconscious. 'Conceptions which arise about the laws of production in the heads of the agents of capitalist production and circulation diverge drastically from these real laws'; and 'individuals have become enslaved under a power alien to them'.[1] These conceptions, which did not correspond with reality, were what Marx called 'ideology'. Ideology for Marx was necessarily false consciousness – the false idea of their motives formed by men who were unconscious of the real laws governing their actions. As Engels put it: 'That the material life-conditions of persons inside whose heads the thought process goes on determine in the last resort the course of this process, remains of necessity unknown to these persons, for otherwise there would be an end of all ideology.'[2] What were decisive were the unconscious, not the conscious, motives and actions of those engaged in production. It was only the communists who, in the words of the *Communist Manifesto*, 'have, over the mass of the proletariat,

[1] Marx, *Capital*, 3 307; Marx and Engels, *The German Ideology*, 48.
[2] F. Engels, *Ludwig Feuerbach* (Engl. transl. 1934) 65–6.

the advantage of clearly understanding the line of march'. Marx did not consider it his function to issue positive injunctions – much less to propound a new ideology. His aim was to unmask error and illusion. Marx, following Hegel, identified the historical process with the growth of consciousness, and the growth of consciousness with the growth of freedom. Thus the final revolution leading to the Marxist Utopia of the classless society would also mean the ending of the rift between reality and ideology, and the realization of true freedom and true consciousness.

This belief in the liberating character of the understanding, traduced and caricatured in the aphorism that 'freedom is the recognition of necessity', gave Marx a place in two worlds. He was primarily concerned with analysis. But analysis was a condition of therapy. Marx was the real founder of the social sciences, in which man is both the object of investigation and the investigator; and man cannot investigate himself without changing himself. Marx looked forward to 'the full development of man's control over the forces of nature – including his own nature'.[1] Marx, however, who lived in a world where the supremacy of the individual entrepreneur and the climate of *laissez-faire* had not yet been seriously disturbed, could not fully emancipate himself from the iron laws of classical economics: these continued to dominate his thinking. The period between the death of Marx and the Russian revolution witnessed a rapid transition. Freud, like Marx, uncovered the reality that lay behind unconscious behaviour. Freud, like Marx, rejected the assumption of an unchanging human nature. But analysis was subordinated to therapy. Science became more specifically instrumental. The aim was no longer to ascertain objective facts, but to establish working hypotheses which led to positive results; human behaviour and human impulses are moulded by means which can be studied and applied by psychiatrists. What Freud did was to add a new dimension to reason. Reason can investigate, understand and utilize the irrational.

The Russian revolution stands on the highroad of this transi-

[1] K. Marx, *Pre-Capitalist Economic Formations*, ed. E. Hobsbawm (1964) 84.

tion. Lenin remained formally within the Marxist framework. But, while the *Communist Manifesto* had counted on 'the gradual, spontaneous class organization of the proletariat', Lenin treated 'spontaneity' as the bane of the Russian workers' movement and as the converse of 'consciousness'. Socialism was a more rational method of organizing the productive process than capitalism precisely because it was 'conscious'. For Marx, communist consciousness arises only when 'an alteration of men on a mass scale' takes place, i.e. by a revolution.[1] In Lenin's scheme a highly conscious elite party was needed to bring revolutionary consciousness to the mass of workers. Marx believed that the new man would arise 'spontaneously' out of the new society; Lenin realized that it was necessary to create the new man in order to create the new society. With the recognition of this need, the word 'ideology' changed its meaning. Ideology for Lenin was no longer necessarily false consciousness. Its character was dependent on its content. Revolutionary or socialist ideology was what the party and its leaders strove to inculcate in the workers. 'Ideology', declares the current Soviet *Philosophical Dictionary*, 'may be a true or a false, a scientific or an unscientific, reflection of reality.'

Lenin remained in one respect rooted in the nineteenth century. While he proclaimed the need to instruct and influence the masses, he continued to believe in instruction by rational persuasion or by force of experience. By the middle of the twentieth century this belief had lost much of its validity both in the Soviet Union and elsewhere. This was perhaps the fundamental difference which marked the transition from Lenin to Stalin. Lenin regarded persuasion or indoctrination as a rational process in the sense that it sought to implant a rational conviction in the minds of those to whom it was directed. Stalin regarded it as a rational process only in the sense that it was planned and conducted by a rational elite. Its aim was to induce large numbers of people to behave in a desired way. How to achieve this aim was a technical problem which was the object of rational study. But the most effective means to employ in achieving this aim did not

[1] Marx and Engels, *The German Ideology*, 86.

always, or not often, appeal to the reason. It would be erroneous to suppose that this transition was peculiar to the USSR, or to any particular form of government. A similar development in western democratic countries has often been attributed to the influence of commercial advertising, the techniques of which, and sometimes the practitioners who applied them, were transferred from the commercial world to that of politics. The candidate is sold to the voter by the same means used to sell patent medicines or refrigerators. The enormous expansion of media of mass communication has clearly also been a factor. But deeper underlying causes have been at work. The professional, politically neutral, public relations consultant, setting out to create a favourable image for his clients and to mould opinion, by every known technical and psychological device, in the sense desired by them, is a now familiar phenomenon, difficult to reconcile with the principles of Lincoln or Gladstone, but apparently inseparable from contemporary mass democracy. The future of democracy, in any part of the world, is today a disturbing problem. Here, as in other respects, the transition from liberal democracy to mass democracy in the western world has reflected the experience of the Russian revolution.

* * *

The other phenomenon of the modern world in which the Russian revolution has played a significant part has been the movement for the liberation of the so-called backward peoples. In the aftermath of the French revolution, the proposition that one man is as good as another was extended to the proposition that one nation is as good as another. Equality of rights for individuals was held to include equality of rights for nations, and the liberation of nations became a purpose as vital, and as intoxicating, as the liberation of man. This conception remained as one of the most durable legacies of the French revolution to the nineteenth and twentieth centuries. Marx, though he postulated the ultimate goal of a world without nations as well as without classes, regarded the liberation of subject nations as a milestone on the road to revolution, and as a cause worthy of the support of radicals and revolutionaries; he was himself concerned in particular with the wrongs of the Irish and the Poles. While, however, some attention was given, by Marx and by others, to the problems of India and China, the nineteenth century scarcely thought of the undeveloped peoples of Asia and Africa as candidates for nationhood and liberation. Nationalism remained primarily a European phenomenon, and could be fitted by Marxist thinkers into the scheme of successive bourgeois and proletarian revolutions. As Lenin put it, the proletariat, as the oppressed class which possessed no rights, was the natural 'standard-bearer of all peoples in the struggle for liberty'.[1]

These attitudes were profoundly affected by the intensive commercial and political penetration of other continents by the European Powers which occupied the last quarter of the nineteenth century, and came to be known by the generic term 'imperialism'. It is difficult to dissociate this process from the broad wave of prosperity enjoyed by the capitalist economies of western Europe at the turn of the century. But, though imperialism seemed in the short run to have brought a powerful reinforcement to capitalism, it could also be seen from another angle as the Achilles' heel of the capitalist Powers. In the decade before 1917, both Rosa Luxemburg and Lenin were heavily preoccupied with the question of imperialism. Differences between them existed, and were magnified in later polemics. But both agreed in regarding imperialism as the last fling of capitalism in decline; and anything that served to sap and destroy imperialism would therefore hasten the downfall of capitalism. All socialists feared and expected that imperialist policies would lead sooner or later to war between the Great Powers, and believed in theory that war would spell the downfall of capitalism; Rosa Luxemburg, Lenin and every Bolshevik looked forward to the war as providing a heaven-sent opportunity to work actively for this result.

This picture had, however, its reverse side. The prosperity of capitalism in its imperialist phase had an important, though at

[1] Lenin, *Polnoe Sobranie Sochinenii*, 5th ed. v 334.

first unnoticed, by-product: the growth of 'revisionism' in the German Social-Democratic Party and of similar tendencies in other socialist and labour parties of western Europe. The grievances of the workers had become less acute. The prospect loomed large of mitigating them further by peaceful pressure on governments, or by bargains and compromises with them. To use democratic procedures in order to influence, to control, and perhaps eventually to take over, governments began to make sense. The entry of an isolated socialist into a French bourgeois government in 1900 created a scandal in the French socialist movement. But this act evidently paved the way for socialist-controlled French governments in the future. The first successes of British labour on the parliamentary scene belonged to the same period. The view that all reforms under a capitalist regime were illusory was sharply challenged by the view that a peaceful revolution was possible. In western countries, the Marxist programme of the overthrow of capitalist governments was relegated to a distant future, and had no apparent relevance to the present.

These developments had no counterpart in eastern Europe, and Lenin continued to bask in the illusion that revisionism had been soundly defeated in the west. His discovery in August 1914 of the extent to which the workers' parties of western Europe had identified themselves with their national governments convinced him of the need to build a new international movement from the foundations. This was attempted at Zimmerwald in 1915. The unexpected victory of the Russian revolution provided a solid national base for the attempt. The sectarian Zimmerwald movement was replaced by a world-wide organization for the overthrow of capitalism: the Third or Communist International. Had the Russian revolution been quickly followed – as the Bolsheviks at first expected – by revolutions in western Europe, its priority would have been no more than a chronological anomaly in the total scheme. But when the cause of revolution, having proved barren in the west, flourished in the fertile soil of Asia, the shape of things to come radically changed. The abortive Russian revolution of 1905 had appeared to provide an impulse, in the ensuing

years, for revolutions in Turkey, Persia and China. The extension
to other continents of a movement for national liberation hitherto
confined mainly to Europe was the most conspicuous international
achievement of the revolution of 1917. In Central Asia, in Persia,
Turkey and Egypt and throughout the Middle East, Soviet
Russia seemed the natural ally of the underdog against the arch-
imperialist Power, Great Britain. In India and Afghanistan the
nationalist movement looked naturally to Moscow; in China
Soviet Russia won prestige and sympathy as the first Power which
voluntarily abandoned extra-territorial rights. As the revolutions
of 1789 and 1848 spread from France, not to England, but eastward to less advanced countries of central Europe, so the Russian
revolution spread, not westward into Europe, but eastward into
the less advanced Asian continent. The revolution could now be
seen not only as a revolt against bourgeois capitalism in the most
backward western country, but as a revolt against western imperialism in the most advanced eastern country. Lenin, in the
last article he ever wrote, consoled himself for the failure of the
revolution in Europe with the reflection that 'the east has already
entered the revolutionary movement' and that 'Russia, India,
China etc. contribute a huge majority of the population of the
world'.[1] It was a dramatic touch of Lenin's old insight. The torch
of revolution, abandoned by western Europe, had been taken up
by peoples of Asia and Africa formerly dependent, in name or in
fact, on the European Powers. The changed shape of the world
today, and the changed relations between western Europe and the
advanced English-speaking countries on the one hand, and the
rest of the world on the other, are a tribute to the historical
significance of the Russian revolution.

Much more, however, was involved in the change than a mere
geographical transposition. The Marxist revolution reached the
peoples of Asia and Africa in its Leninist incarnation. Industrial-
-ization had to be pursued in these countries in conditions far

[1] Lenin, *Polnoe Sobranie Sochinenii*, 5th ed. xlv 404; a few weeks earlier he had
written: 'Our European philistines do not dream that the future revolutions in
countries of the east . . . will display undoubtedly greater peculiarities than the
Russian revolution.' (Ibid. 381.)

closer to those experienced in the Soviet Union than to those envisaged by Marx. The victory of a proletarian revolution in predominantly peasant Russia was explained by Lenin as a provisional stage, at the end of which the mass of poorer peasants would have been assimilated to a proletariat. What happened in Russia in October 1917 could still be plausibly called a proletarian revolution, though not in the full Marxist sense. But in China the predominantly peasant character and leadership of the revolution was undisguised; and in many undeveloped countries a proletariat was altogether lacking. More significant still was the weakness, or sometimes total absence, of a bourgeoisie or of any of the concepts of a bourgeois society. In these countries, the bourgeois revolution, still unfinished in the Russia of 1917, had not even begun. Here the Russian problem was reproduced in an extreme form, and could be met only by the Leninist solution of a small intellectual elite to assume the leadership of the revolution. Many of these new leaders had received their education, and made their first acquaintance with Marxism, in western countries or under western auspices. But, in practice, local conditions made Marxism applicable only in its Leninist transformation. The absence of a bourgeoisie and of an established bourgeois tradition meant the rejection, in practice if not in theory, of bourgeois liberal democracy and a return to Rousseauistic or Jacobin conceptions of democracy; and the influence of the USSR appeared in many of these countries to predominate over that of the west.

This predominance is, however, not unqualified. The revolt of nationalism against imperialism has almost everywhere succeeded in winning political independence. But this has made the persistence of an unavoidable economic dependence all the more galling and inspires constant complaints of 'neo-colonialism'. The example of the USSR, which, thanks to its natural resources and by gigantic efforts, made itself economically independent of the west, excites envy and admiration. But all these countries, with the exception of China, know that such a task is beyond their powers. 'Economic aid' has become an indispensable factor of national life. At first it seemed less invidious and less dangerous to receive aid from the Soviet Union than from the west. But gradually consciousness dawned that exclusive economic dependence either on one side or on the other carried a threat to national independence; taunts of Soviet 'colonialism' or 'imperialism' did not altogether miss their mark. Hence the policies of 'non-alignment' followed more or less actively by most of these countries, inspired partly by a desire to obtain aid from both sides, and partly by a desire to maintain a maximum degree of independence. In China non-alignment has been extended to the point of acute hostility to both camps.

It is perhaps too early to attempt to place these ambiguous events in historical perspective. What is clear is that the Russian revolution has triggered off a revolutionary movement of revolt in Asia and Africa against the nineteenth-century capitalist order, in which the challenge is directed not against the exploitation of the industrial workers of the advanced countries, but against the exploitation of backward colonial peoples. It never occurred to Lenin, and was never admitted later, that a revolution under these auspices, while it might be directed against capitalism, and have aims that could be described as socialist, had moved far away from the Marxist premises. The post-Leninist re-orientation of the socialist revolution implied that the final overthrow of capitalism would be the work not of its proletarian victims in the advanced countries (who had somehow become its allies), but of its colonial victims in the undeveloped countries, and that it would be the work not of an economic class, but of a political movement. The era of the French revolution ended in 1917, and a new revolutionary epoch opened. Historians of the future may debate whether that epoch ended in 1949, when the Asian and African revolution effectively began, or whether these events can be interpreted as a slightly unorthodox prolongation of the Russian revolution. Such debates about what is called 'periodization' are not very fruitful, and it is unnecessary to anticipate them. But, so long as man is interested in exploring his past, nobody will doubt the credentials of the revolution of 1917 as one of the great turning-points in his history.

II 'What is to be Done?'

THE author of *What is to be Done?*, Nikolai Gavrilovich Cherny-shevsky, was a typical member – one might even say, *the* typical member – of the Russian revolutionary intelligentsia of the second half of the nineteenth century. He was dogmatic and self-assured, self-sacrificing to the point of quixotry, earnest to the point of humourlessness, a fervent believer in the power of reason and of ideas, but also prepared for any action, however reckless and far-reaching, which seemed rationally designed to promote the great cause of progress. He was the son of a priest – this also was a characteristic trait – and was born in 1828 in the Volga town of Saratov. At the age of eighteen he found his way to the University of Petersburg, and there he witnessed from afar the European revolutions of 1848, which were the turning-point in his life and in his beliefs. From then on, he became a dedicated radical and revolutionary.

After a brief period as a teacher Chernyshevsky turned to a literary career, and from 1854 onward was one of the regular and most effective contributors to the progressive journal *Sovremennik* (*The Contemporary*), Belinsky's old organ. The moment was propitious. The death of Nicholas I in 1855 and the relaxation of censorship and repression which marked the first years of Alex-ander II enabled Chernyshevsky to abandon the literary and aesthetic essays, which were the first cloak for his advanced opinions, for the open discussion of the crucial problems of agrarian policy and of the peasant commune. Presently he became involved in the organization of underground activities. In the fresh wave of reaction which followed the proclamation of the emancipation of the serfs he was arrested in 1862. For more than eighteen months he remained in the Peter-and-Paul fortress; and it was here that he wrote *What is to be Done?* In 1864 – the year in which the novel was published – he was sent to hard labour in Siberia, where he remained till 1883. Then he was allowed to live in Astrakhan, and eventually – a few months before his death in 1889 – to return to his native town of Saratov. During this long postscript to his active political life he continued to record his impressions in letters and diaries, and even occasionally for publication. But the important part of his literary career is concentrated in the years 1853 to 1862, with *What is to be Done?* as its culminating point.

Chernyshevsky marked the transition from the group known in nineteenth-century Russian intellectual history as 'the men of the forties' to 'the men of the sixties', of whom he could claim to have been the first. 'The men of the forties' – Bakunin, Herzen, Ogarev, Turgenev, Belinsky, with all their differences, all belonged to this group – were in essence members of the last generation of the Romantics. Politically, they were reared in the tradition of constitutional western liberalism; philosophically, in the tradition of the German idealists, mainly Fichte, Schelling and Hegel. Reacting against the backwardness, the harshness, and the obscurantism of the Russia of the Tsars, finding their lodestar in an idealized picture of the liberty, equality, and fraternity of the west, they failed to evolve any concrete programme, whether of reform or of revolution, for their own country. They often seemed to be concerned more with individual self-improvement than with the reconstruction of Russian society, which was abandoned or neglected as a hopeless task. The derisive label applied to them by 'the men of the sixties' which stuck most closely was 'the cult of the beautiful soul'.

The European revolutions of 1848–49 were the dividing-line between the two Russian generations. Except for Belinsky, who died in Russia in 1847, all the important 'men of the forties' had gone to western Europe as temporary or permanent *émigrés*.

Bakunin, arrested in Saxony, spent more than ten vital years in the dungeons of three countries and in Siberia, and reappeared in western Europe only after the new lines of demarcation had been drawn. Only Herzen and Turgenev remained to defend in their different ways the outmoded tradition of the forties against the challenge of the younger generation.

Chernyshevsky had begun his public career as an ardent admirer and disciple of Herzen. At the end of the 1850s when Herzen accepted at its face value the 'thaw' of the first years of Alexander's reign and seemed ready to come to terms with the reforming autocrat, the breach occurred between Herzen and Chernyshevsky which marked the opening of hostilities between the generations. Herzen in a famous article of 1859 in his London journal *The Bell*, under the title (in English) 'Very Dangerous!!', criticized the intransigent radicalism of Chernyshevsky and his friends in Russia. A visit by Chernyshevsky to Herzen in London only hardened the antipathy between them. Nor did it improve matters when, after the emancipation of the serfs in 1861 and the Polish insurrection two years later, Herzen was forced to admit that the reforming zeal of Alexander II had been skin-deep, and had barely touched the surface of the autocracy. By this time the rift between the cautious liberals of the forties and the angry young radicals of the sixties was too deep to be bridged.

The men of the sixties proudly thought of themselves as rejecting sentimental romanticism for hard-headed realism, philosophical idealism for materialism, metaphysics for science. Though the ideas of the western European Enlightenment had penetrated Russian court circles under Catherine the Great, they had made little impact on Russian life or on Russian politics; and the cult of reason which played so fundamental a role in Chernyshevsky's thinking was in some respects only a belated afterglow of the vision which had dawned on France and western Europe in the eighteenth century. Helvétius, Diderot and Rousseau – the Rousseau of *Émile* and *La Nouvelle Héloïse* rather than of the *Confessions* and the *Social Contract* – were among Chernyshevsky's early gods. The intellectual movement of the 1860s had some claim to be called Russia's Age of Reason.

But it was Reason cast in a new mould. This was preeminently the age of the supreme cult of science. Chernyshevsky had been an early Russian devotee of Feuerbach ('man ist was man isst'). It was that once famous bible of materialism, Büchner's *Kraft und Stoff*, published in Germany in 1855 and quickly circulated in Russia in illicit translations, which satisfied the young Russians of the 1860s that human life and human behaviour were to be explained in material and physiological terms, and that the reform of society was in the strictest sense a scientific problem. Rather surprisingly, Chernyshevsky dismissed Comte as superficial, and was shocked by the deductions which some social thinkers were beginning to draw from Darwin's survival of the fittest. But this was because he felt himself to possess a simpler and more direct key to the problems of society. The question of morality seemed to him to have been solved once for all by the English Utilitarians, known to him principally through John Stuart Mill, whom he translated. Nothing else could be expected, and nothing else was needed, than the pursuit by every individual of his rational and enlightened self-interest. Like Buckle, Chernyshevsky attributed misconduct to ignorance.

The use of fiction for the discussion and dissemination of social ideas was already a Russian nineteenth-century tradition. Herzen in the forties, before his departure from Russia, had written a short and not very successful novel, *Who is to Blame?*, which attempted to analyse the eternal triangle in the naïve terms of a rational morality. In 1862 Turgenev, quickly sensitive to the appearance on the scene of the young men of the sixties, had introduced a caricature of one of them, under the name Bazarov, into his novel *Fathers and Sons*, applying to him, and putting into popular circulation for the first time, the title of 'nihilist'. Bazarov is the classic example of the type: indeed, one may suspect that this is a case where a caricature of genius helped to create the type. Bazarov constantly insists on his mission: he is a man dedicated to a cause – 'no ordinary man'. His creed is science plus rational morality: he 'does not believe in principles, but believes in frogs', and thinks that 'a decent chemist is twenty times more useful than any poet'. Chernyshevsky's *What is to be Done?* is not so much a retort to *Fathers and Sons* as a proud acceptance of it. His principal characters are reincarnations of Bazarov. Lopukhóv spurns 'what are called lofty feelings, ideal impulses', and exalts 'the striving of every man for his own advantage'. Kirsánov (the very name is borrowed from Turgenev) treats 'pompous words like honour' as 'ambiguous and obscure', and proclaims that 'every man is an egoist'. Rakhmétov, introduced in a chapter entitled 'An Unusual Man', eats beef to make himself strong, sleeps on nails to harden himself for the tasks ahead, and, like Bazarov, adopts a deliberately brusque manner of conversation lest he should waste time unnecessarily on empty words and formalities.

Almost everything about *What is to be Done?* is disconcerting to the western reader. Its form is that of a highly discursive Victorian English novel. Its original subtitle, *Tales about New People*, should warn the reader against expecting a single unitary plot. It wanders from theme to theme, minor characters appear and disappear, new major characters are suddenly introduced at the whim of the author. The one character who runs throughout the story, and round whom the action revolves, is the heroine, Véra Pávlovna; but three-quarters of the way through, a secondary heroine (with her attendant hero) appears in the person of Katerina, and for some time occupies the centre of the stage. If symmetry and order were essential qualities of art, *What is to be Done?* could not be ranked as a work of art. The author holds conversations with the 'perceptive reader', buttonholing him in the distressingly arch manner of Thackeray, whom he more than once quotes with admiration (an admiration tempered by the just criticism of sameness and lack of breadth – everything that he has to say is in *Vanity Fair*, and the rest mere repetition). But he does not even pick up the scattered threads of his story in the last chapter with the formal tidiness of the Victorian novelist. (It ends in a bewildering and incomprehensible Walpurgis Night of Reason, with a nameless Woman in Black leading the abstemious revels, and in the half-mocking promise of a second part – which was, of course, never written. This material is omitted from the present edition.)

The other disconcerting factor for the contemporary reader is Chernyshevsky's attitude to a question which has become the predominant obsession of the mid-twentieth-century western novelist. The Victorian novelist, like Victorian society, veiled the physical relations between the sexes in a cloud of prudery. But neither he nor his reader for a moment questioned their importance; they were merely transposed by the convention of the period into a sentimental key. The attitude of Chernyshevsky is quite different. He does not mince his words when he brings on to the stage a reformed prostitute or the mistress of a rich man. But in a book which is constantly – one might almost say, primarily – concerned with the relation, and specifically the marital relation, between men and women, he dismisses the physical aspect of that relation as unessential and not seriously worth discussion. He had already made his standpoint clear in a review of Turgenev's story 'Asia': 'Away with erotic problems. The modern reader has no interest in them. He is concerned with the question of perfecting the administration and the judicial system, with financial questions, with the problem of liberating the peasant.'

The descriptions of life in *What is to be Done?* lead us to suppose that Véra Pávlovna has no physical relations with her first husband, Lopukhóv, such relations being incompatible with their rational conception of human behaviour. Certain passages might support the inference that she and her second husband, Kirsánov, conducted themselves more normally. But Chernyshevsky nowhere makes this point explicit, as he would have done if he had thought it important; and it would be a complete anachronism to seek here an explanation of the breakdown of Vera's first marriage. Another strange feature of *What is to be Done?* comes into the picture at this point. In the endless discussions about marriage in which Véra Pávlovna and her two successive partners engage, no hint occurs anywhere that marriage commonly results in offspring or that this may be one of its functions. The leading characters of the novel have parents, but no children. In one place only, in reporting a conversation of the secondary heroine Katerina a few years after her marriage in which she casually mentions her son, the author adds, without further elaboration, in an almost comic parenthesis: 'So she has a son.' So passionate a believer as Chernyshevsky in the future of the human race must have wanted and expected children to be produced. But he would clearly have liked them to be produced in some way which impinged less disturbingly on the rational human personality. All this creates an embarrassing impression of lack not only of sophistication but also of common sense, especially when Chernyshevsky describes his characters diverting themselves in harmless merriment. Again and again the reader is tempted to exclaim in the language of Byron:

O Mirth and Innocence! O Milk and Water!

But the Russian revolutionaries were not innocents abroad, and were anything but milk-and-water characters. What was the inspiration which they found in *What is to be Done?*; and what made it for more than fifty years a major revolutionary classic? It is not easy to label Chernyshevsky. A nihilist he was certainly not – except in the sense that every Russian radical and progressive believed automatically in the total destruction of the existing order of Russian society. Chernyshevsky is generally counted as a narodnik or 'populist' (to use the conventional English equivalent); for that term covers a wealth of different ideas and a chaotic, amorphous movement of revolt. But Chernyshevsky lacked the idealization of the Russian peasant commune which was often regarded as the hallmark of 'populism'. He was more interested in the town than in the country; and this has helped to establish the picture of him in current Soviet tradition as an embryonic Russian Marxist. Nor does Chernyshevsky show anything of the common desire of the populists to glorify Russia at the expense of the bourgeois and decadent west. He had no Slavophile leanings and remained, in terms of Russian thought, an unrepentant westerner. The keynotes of all his writing, and what succeeding generations of revolutionaries above all found in him, were faith in socialism, faith in progress, and faith in reason.

Socialism was the term which all Russian radicals, from Herzen onward, applied to their vision of the society of the future. Negatively, it carried with it the firm rejection of western bourgeois democracy and western capitalism. Positively, early Russian socialism was nourished on the imaginary societies and commonwealths of the French utopians, of whom Fourier, with his 'phalansteries' and his psychological speculations about the transformation of human nature, was the most popular and influential in Russia. In a country where any kind of political activity was taboo, socialism long remained in its utopian and purely imaginative stage. The economic background of *What is to be Done?* is provided by the co-operatives of seamstresses formed by the heroine and described in loving detail. From the socialist economy the features of profit, competition and exploitation inherent in capitalism will disappear; and the welfare of the new community will be solidly built on equal co-operation and mutual aid among the workers engaged in production. Here Chernyshevsky provides an urban counterpart for the 'going to the people' in the villages which was so characteristic a feature of the populist movement. Two generations of Chernyshevsky's readers were satisfied and inspired by this unsophisticated picture of selfless human endeavour.

Faith in progress and in the ultimate attainment of the goal is common to all the characters in *What is to be Done?* Here, too, Chernyshevsky harks back to the Enlightenment, and may be regarded as the disciple of Condorcet far more than of Darwin. Progress remains for him a basic assumption, an article of belief, rather than something that calls for scientific proof. A pathetic letter written to his wife from Siberia in 1871, after nine years of imprisonment and exile, attests both his faith in the future and his faith in his own mission:

Poor Russian people, a miserable fate awaits it in this struggle. But the result will be favourable, and then, my dear, it will have need of truth. I am no longer a young man, but remember that our life is still ahead of us. . . . I can speak of historical events because I have learned and thought much. My turn will come. We will then see whether it is worth complaining about the fact that for so many years I have only been able to study and think. We will then see that this has been useful for our country.[1]

But, most of all, it is faith in human reason which served as the *leitmotiv* of *What is to be Done?* and as the inspiration which drove men and women to do and to suffer in the sacred cause of the revolution. Reason had given man the power to master and transform his material environment: the wonders of science were unbounded. But reason, it now seemed clear, had also given man the power to transform himself and, in transforming himself, to transform society. Like most Russians, Chernyshevsky was not an individualist in the sense of setting up any sharp opposition between society and the individual: to transform one meant to transform the other. When Chernyshevsky speaks of the 'new men' he is thinking also of the new society which they will build.

The theme of the 'new men' runs as a guiding thread through the pages of *What is to be Done?* Six years ago, remarks Chernyshevsky with odd precision, the new type of man did not yet exist. His predecessors (these are still 'the men of the forties') 'felt themselves alone, powerless, and were therefore inactive, or despondent, or exalted, or indulged in romanticism and fantasy'. The new man is marked by 'cold-blooded practicality, regular and calculating activity, active calculation'. The characters in *What is to be Done?* are 'new men' carried, as we have seen, to the extreme point of logical consistency. The heroine, Véra Pávlovna, is 'one of the first women whose life has been ordered well'. These people were the harbingers of the new society. At present there were still ten 'antediluvians' to one modern man. But 'the number of decent people grows every year', and soon 'all people will be decent people'.

[1] Quoted from F. Venturi, *Roots of Revolution* (New York 1960) 184. This work contains the best recent account of Chernyshevsky in English.

The faith and optimism of Chernyshevsky are thus simpler, more direct, and more naïve than the faith and optimism of Marx. Marx believed in the forces of history working themselves out through the actions of men to a goal that could be foreseen. This, too, was belief in reason, but in a less personal reason than that which occupied the central place in Chernyshevsky's thought. For Chernyshevsky it was human ignorance rather than the interested resistance of those in possession which was the ultimate obstacle to progress. But this conviction also brought a message of hope. The task of the revolutionaries was to instruct and transform human beings, to make 'decent people' of them, by persuading them to harken to the voice of reason.

There is no doubt about the potency of this message in the time and circumstances in which it was delivered. Even Turgenev, who complained that Chernyshevsky did not 'understand poetry', admitted that he understood 'the needs of real contemporary life'. It was Chernyshevsky more than any other one man who shaped the moral attitudes of two generations of Russian revolutionaries. Lenin hailed him as 'a great Russian socialist' (though still a 'utopian socialist') and undoubtedly regarded him as one of the precursors of Bolshevism. Lenin's ideal revolutionary would have lived as Chernyshevsky's heroes and heroines lived. It should not be forgotten that Chernyshevsky's one novel was written in prison in the first year of his long martyrdom for his convictions. These grim surroundings were the birthplace not only of *What is to be Done?* but also of the whole revolutionary movement. It is neither accidental nor surprising that this grey, austere, humourless Utopia – a reflection of these conditions – should have set the tone for the human and personal side of the revolution.

III *Red Rosa*

ROSA LUXEMBURG is a proper subject for a full-length biography; and Mr Nettl's two volumes are the first thorough and
scholarly attempt to do justice to this amazing and dramatic
career.[1] In the 1890s she was a key figure in the development of
Polish socialism; for twenty years before her assassination in
January 1919 she was a focus of every issue and every controversy in the ranks of German Social-Democracy; she consorted
on equal terms with Lenin on the platform of the Second International; she wrote one of the very few (half a dozen at most)
critiques of Marxist economic doctrine which still have to be
taken into account; hers was the most eloquent and influential
voice raised from the Left in Germany against the First World
War; she played a leading, though ultimately ineffectual, role in
the founding of the German Communist Party. No single country
can claim her; no party – not even the German Communist
Party which she helped to found – pays unqualified homage to
her memory; her status in the corpus of socialist writers as a
Marxist who challenged Marx on a point of economic theory is
anomalous.

Yet the strength of the impression which she made on her
contemporaries and fellow-workers is universally attested. Her
unique success lay perhaps in her capacity to combine the spirit
of compassion, of indignation at the unmerited sufferings inflicted by a callous social system, which was the ultimate force
behind socialism as a crusading doctrine, with a cool and rigorous

[1] J. P. Nettl, *Rosa Luxemburg* (1966) 2 vols.

intellectual analysis of the conditions in which that system flourished and through which it would eventually perish. The fundamental humanitarianism of Rosa Luxemburg's outlook was the source of her strength. In one sense, too, it may have been a source of weakness. For, while Rosa Luxemburg reached early in life an intellectual conviction that revolution was necessary and justifiable, and acted on that conviction throughout her career, she never fully faced the element of ruthlessness which seems to enter into every revolution in action. It is at any rate arguable that the German revolution failed because its leaders were less ruthless than those who set out to strangle and crush it.

Rosa Luxemburg was the child of a middle-class Jewish family in a small Polish town, where she was born in 1870. She was never physically strong, and some hip disease in childhood left her slightly lame. Her assets, apart from her quick and powerful intelligence, were a beautiful voice and capacity to hold and sway a large audience. She had her schooling in Warsaw – naturally in Russian; and, having become early involved in revolutionary activities, she was smuggled out of Poland at the age of eighteen to continue her studies in the university of Zürich. For the next ten years she led the life of the young international revolutionary in exile. She played a prominent part in 1893 in splitting the Polish Socialist Party (PPS) – the party which was one day to provide an ideological platform for Pilsudski's fascist state, and which was already guilty of the heresy of rating Polish national claims to independence higher than the international solidarity of the workers. She was one of the leaders of the new party which, flaunting its indifference to Polish national unity, confined its activities to Russian Poland, called itself 'the Social-Democracy of the Kingdom of Poland', and was later, in defiance of traditional Polish hatred of Russia, to affiliate itself to the Russian Social-Democratic Party. Rosa Luxemburg, by way of reaction against extravagant Polish nationalism, remained a thorough-going internationalist and enemy of all national pretensions. She afterwards crossed swords with Lenin on the issue of national self-determination, sharing the same point of view with Radek and several leading Bolsheviks, and after the Russian revolution severely criticized the toleration shown by Lenin to Ukrainian separatism.

So long as the Tsar reigned, Poland was a barren and dangerous ground for revolutionaries; and from 1898 onwards Rosa Luxemburg was active in Germany, going through a formal marriage ceremony with a German in order to avoid the risk of expulsion. It was the moment when the German Social-Democratic Party was being torn by the controversy over 'revisionism' – the campaign of Bernstein and others to 'revise' Marxism in the sense of admitting that the aims of the workers could be achieved by reform more effectively than by revolution, by using the machinery of the bourgeois state rather than by seeking to destroy it. Rosa threw herself heart and soul into the defence of Marxism, whole and undefiled by compromise; no other path but revolution could lead the proletariat to its goal. Bourgeois democracy could never become the instrument for the achievement of socialism. Rosa Luxemburg's first important book, *Social Reform or Revolution?*, which originally appeared as articles in the party press, was the outcome of this controversy. Bernstein's programme was to 'change the ocean of capitalist bitterness into a sweet socialist sea by pouring in individual bottles full of social reformist lemonade'. She was equally hostile to the conciliatory tactics of Jaurès in France, and, *a fortiori*, to the participation of French socialists in bourgeois governments. There was plenty in her record, even before the anti-war agitation of the pre-war and war years, to justify the sobriquet 'Red Rosa'.

This uncompromising advocacy of revolution led her into a hotly contested argument with the trade unions. She told the German trade union leader Legien that he was 'childish, and had no idea of the real circumstances of revolution', and denounced 'the old arthritic English conception that trade unions can prosper only through peaceful growth and development'. The attitude of Marx and his disciples to trade-unionism always had in it a streak of ambivalence. Trade unions, said Marx, were necessary and vital 'so long as capitalism exists'. But their primary pre-occupation was to make the best of things for the workers under capitalism, and this always carried with it the risk of being diverted from the essential aim and purpose of overthrowing capitalism. The trade unions were always tempted to treat the issue as an economic struggle between workers and employers and neglect its political aspects: Lenin often used the English word 'trade-unionism' contemptuously in this sense. In the early 1900s this controversy became acute in Germany, where the trade unions and the Social-Democratic Party were always to some extent rivals for the allegiance of the workers. For Rosa Luxemburg, as for Lenin, the party always came first. In 1906 she wrote a famous pamphlet under the title *The Mass Strike, the Party and the Trade Unions*, in which, influenced in part by the events of the Russian revolution of 1905, she defended the general strike as a revolutionary weapon and denounced the desire of the trade unions to reserve the strike as a weapon in the economic struggle against the employers. The German trade unions were, in her view, deeply imbued with the heresy of revisionism; and her bitter taunts and strictures at this time won her the deep-seated animosity of the trade union hierarchy.

The Accumulation of Capital, originally published in 1913, needs to be read as a broadside in Rosa Luxemburg's long campaign in the defence of the cause of revolution against the 'revisionists'. Its edge and purpose cannot indeed be fully appreciated except in this context; and, while the English translation seems excellent,[1] it is perhaps a pity that the introduction should have been entrusted, not to someone familiar with the international socialist movement who could have filled in the historical background of the work, but to a distinguished economist who embarks on the task of examining its relevance to current academic economic theory. In writing it the author never strayed far from her main preoccupation, which was to refute the

---

[1] R. Luxemburg, *The Accumulation of Capital*, with an introduction by Joan Robinson (1951).

'revisionists' who wanted to do a deal with the capitalist state, and to reassure the faint-hearted who were tempted to believe that, after all, capitalism had within it powers of survival which would enable it to last for ever.

With this end in view Rosa Luxemburg sought not merely to reinforce the verdict of Marx that capitalism was doomed to perish through its own inherent contradictions, but to close a loophole which Marx seemed inadvertently to have left open. The second volume of *Capital* had been written up by Engels after Marx's death from the master's notes and drafts, which on certain points were notoriously incomplete. Rosa Luxemburg argued that Marx had failed to demonstrate beyond all manner of doubt why capitalism, by process of progressive accumulation, could not go on expanding for ever; and, so long as expansion was possible, there was no reason why capitalism should not go on. Rosa thought she had found the answer to this unanswered question in the fact that capitalism could continue to expand only for so long as it could find non-capitalist – i.e. colonial – markets, and that, as these markets were gradually used up and absorbed into the all-conquering and all-pervading capitalist system, capitalism itself was bound to decline and ultimately collapse.

Rosa Luxemburg's argument was found convincing by some German economists; but *The Accumulation of Capital* has clearly owed its appeal less to its economic analysis than to the fervour of the political faith that shone through it and to the vigour and brilliance of its indictment of imperialism. The theory which Lenin developed a few years later in *Imperialism as the Highest Stage of Capitalism* had some analogies with that of Rosa Luxemburg, though according to this theory, which Lenin derived mainly from Hilferding and Hobson, what capitalism sought in the colonial and semi-colonial countries was not so much markets as fields for lucrative investment.

But Lenin had the advantage over Rosa Luxemburg, in the eyes of Marxists, of merely carrying on Marx's analysis and not challenging it as inadequate; nor did Lenin ever commit himself so far to the doctrine of the inevitable collapse. It was this point on which, paradoxically enough, later Bolsheviks (though not Lenin and Bukharin in their polemics against her economic theories) fastened in their criticisms of *The Accumulation of Capital*. It was the Mensheviks who dwelt on the element of 'inevitability' in the Marxist doctrine in order to support their condemnation of the Bolsheviks for seeming to move farther and faster than was justified by the development of the historical process. Rosa Luxemburg's criticisms of Bolshevism in the last year of her life clearly proved her Menshevik affiliations; *The Accumulation of Capital* provided a foretaste of her Menshevism. The whole pattern seemed to fit together. A work which was written as a passionate plea for revolutionary action was condemned in later Bolshevik literature for its supposed justification of a policy of inaction.

It was not, however, Rosa Luxemburg's economic theories which gave her her outstanding place in the socialist movement or accounted for the veneration in which her name was held by a whole generation of German workers. These things she owed to her fervent opposition to war – and, in particular, to the war of 1914. Before Rosa Luxemburg appeared on the scene, the Second International and the parties forming it had never seriously had to face the question of war. But as the century ended clouds could be discerned in the international firmament – the Fashoda crisis, the Spanish-American war, the South African war. At the Paris congress of the International in 1900 Rosa Luxemburg moved a resolution condemning militarism, which was carried unanimously, perhaps without much realization of its importance. This was the resolution which first committed 'socialist members of parliament' to vote against budgets 'for military or naval purposes or for colonial expeditions'. It was at that time directed mainly against the French, and was prompted in fact by the recent scandal of Millerand's entry into a bourgeois government. It was, however, already clear that, sooner or later, Social-Democratic parties would be compelled to define their attitude to wars in which their countries were engaged.

It still seemed unthinkable to Rosa Luxemburg and to most

consistent and sincere socialists that that attitude could be other than negative. But by the year 1907, when the Second International held its congress in Stuttgart, and war in Europe was already more than a theoretical possibility, the embarrassments of the question had become plain enough. At that time the 'Social-Democracy of the Kingdom of Poland', whose mandate Rosa Luxemburg held, was affiliated to the Russian Social-Democratic Workers' Party, which was enjoying a short-lived interlude of unity and truce between Bolsheviks and Mensheviks. The Russian party's delegation at the Stuttgart congress consisted of Lenin, Martov and Rosa Luxemburg – a unique occasion.

Lenin and Martov apparently allowed Rosa Luxemburg to make the running on a subject which was peculiarly her own, but gave her their solid support. The resolution on the struggle against militarism presented by the veteran German leader Bebel on behalf of the bureau repeated the usual pledge to vote against war budgets, but was otherwise colourless. Rosa Luxemburg on behalf of the Russian delegation offered an amendment which, after some rather shamefaced opposition from the Germans, was accepted in a slightly attenuated form by the congress, and thus became the accepted doctrine of the International. Under this resolution social-democrats were not only to employ every means to prevent war but, should war none the less occur, they were to do their utmost to 'utilize the economic and political crisis caused by the war' in order to bring about the overthrow of the capitalist order – in everything but name a call to civil war. This drastic resolution was re-voted by each subsequent congress of the Second International down to 1914. Rosa Luxemburg continued to conduct an active campaign on the platform and in the party press till, early in 1914, she was sentenced to a year's imprisonment for incitement to mutiny.

Behind this picture of the workers of the world united under the banner of the Second International in resistance to war, the reality was far different. In a world of uniform economic development and opportunities national differences might, as the *Communist Manifesto* had predicted, have progressively disappeared.

But, in a world where development had been highly unequal and privileges unequally shared, divergences were bound to occur in the attitude of workers of different countries. In the advanced countries, notably in Great Britain and Germany, where the workers had attained a relatively high standard of living and a recognized place in the national polity, the pull of national allegiance was strong enough in the first decade of the twentieth century to outweigh class allegiance. In the western European countries pronouncements of leaders of the workers against militarism and war were more and more apt to carry an explicit or implied reservation of the right of national self-defence; and this meant not a return to Marx's own criterion of supporting in any war the side whose victory seemed more likely to further the socialist cause, but a tacit acceptance of the bourgeois liberal distinction, which Marx had always derided, between aggressive and defensive wars. Only in backward Russia, where the workers enjoyed fewest advantages, was the social-democratic movement largely impervious to the call of loyalty to a national government, and did the social-democratic members of the Duma – though with some trepidation – vote against the national war budget. Lenin correctly attributed the immunity of the Russian workers from 'chauvinism' and 'opportunism' to the fact that 'the stratum of privileged workers and employees is with us very weak'.

The outbreak of war in 1914 brought out starkly enough the element of 'chauvinism' in the German socialist movement – an element which had been firmly planted there by Lassalle, and which lip-service to Marxist doctrine had never eradicated. By a large majority the Social-Democratic group in the Reichstag decided to abandon the party principles and vote in favour of the war credits demanded by the Imperial Government. For Germans, and for socialists all over the Continent, the date 4 August 1914 was the date not of the outbreak of war (war had already been in progress with Russia for three days), but of the rallying of the German Social-Democratic Party to the national cause, of its betrayal of the creed of international socialism. This was the starting-point of the last and most vital phase in Rosa Luxemburg's career. Her opposition to war in general now became a specific mission; and, though she spent most of the war years in and out of prison, she became the voice and the symbol of the campaign against it. Her pamphlet *The Crisis of Social-Democracy* published in 1916 over the signature Junius (and often referred to as 'the Junius brochure') was the most stirring and eloquent denunciation of the war to appear in Germany between 1914 and 1918.

In December 1914, a single member of the Social-Democratic group in the Reichstag, Karl Liebknecht, registered the first solitary vote against the war budget, and courageously repeated his gesture of protest on several occasions down to 1917 when he was arrested and imprisoned. In 1915 Rosa Luxemburg, Karl Liebknecht and a handful of left-wing intellectuals began to issue a series of occasional and illicit anti-war pamphlets which they called 'the Spartacus letters', and from this the group came to be known as the *Spartakusbund*. The success of these leaflets revealed the strength of the latent opposition to the war, which increased as the slaughter dragged on without prospect of end or result. In 1916 there was a breakaway within the Social-Democratic Party, and the Independent Social-Democratic Party was formed with a programme of bringing the war to an end. The *Spartakusbund* was a group within the Independent party. But the difference between them was that the Spartakists were revolutionaries who, like Lenin, wished to use the war as a means to social revolution, whereas the majority of the Independents were merely opposed to the war, some through revolutionary conviction, some through pacifism, and some through sheer war-weariness – a variety of moods similar to that which inspired the Independent Labour Party in Great Britain. The distinction between Spartakists and Independents mattered little so long as the war continued, but became vital immediately after the armistice.

Karl Liebknecht was released in October 1918, when the armistice negotiations began. Rosa Luxemburg remained in prison till the armistice was actually signed. By that time Germany was in the full flood of revolution. Soviets of Workers' and Soldiers' Deputies sprang up in all the large centres; and the supreme authority was a Council of People's Commissars, consisting of three Social-Democrats and three Independent Social-Democrats. The creation of a German Communist Party to clinch the proletarian revolution in Germany and join hands with the Russian revolution became a burning question. In the mind of that ardent and uncritical tribune of the people, Liebknecht, no shadow of doubt on this question could arise. Rosa Luxemburg seems to have hesitated, and wondered whether the mass of the German workers were yet ripe for revolution. But she, too, was carried along with the tide, drafted the programme for the new German Communist Party (which retained the title *Spartakusbund* in parentheses after its name), and was the principal orator at its founding congress in Berlin on the last day of the year 1918.

By this time other forces had begun to assert themselves. In the anarchy of the first weeks after the armistice, when rival groups of armed men were constantly clashing and sometimes fighting pitched battles in the streets of Berlin, the Social-Democratic leaders, with the tacit – or not so tacit – support of what was left of the Army command, were gradually asserting their authority; their programme was to restore order, to break the Soviets and hold elections to a national assembly. By the end of the year they had edged the Independents out of the Council of People's Commissars. By this time it had become uncertain who was in real authority – the generals or the commissars. After the end of the year the street fighting grew more intense and concentrated, and gradually changed its character. The Army and the police had regained their confidence; the initiative was in their hands, no longer in that of the revolutionaries; they were out not merely to restore order but to crush their enemies. Among these the Communists were the first, though not the only, victims. On 15 January 1919, Rosa Luxemburg and Karl Liebknecht were arrested and murdered a few hours later by their captors in circumstances of the utmost brutality. Their

memory was long celebrated by revolutionaries of many countries
as martyrs of the revolution.

The tragedy of Rosa Luxemburg's death was more than personal: it marked the defeat of the ideals for which she had lived.
Much controversy has raged round her attitude to the Bolshevik
revolution. When the split between Bolsheviks and Mensheviks
divided the Russian Social-Democratic Party in 1903 on the issue
of Lenin's insistence on a closely organized and rigidly disciplined
party, it was Rosa Luxemburg who penned the most detailed and
and considered attack on Lenin's 'ultra-centralism', which she
described as bureaucratic rather than democratic, and pointing
inevitably towards an absolutism of the party leadership. Throughout the year which elapsed between the Bolshevik and the German revolutions – from one 'November' to another – she was
behind prison bars, and her opportunities of studying events in
Petrograd and Moscow were correspondingly limited. But she
followed them with intense excitement and anxiety; and some
time after Brest-Litovsk she wrote an essay (there is no sign that
it was revised, or even intended at all, for publication) which
expressed her criticisms and her fears. This essay was published
in an abridged form in 1922 by Paul Levi, who succeeded to the
leadership of the German party after her death but broke with it
and with Moscow in 1921. The intention of the publication was
to discredit Bolshevism; and when the full text was eventually
published five years later the effect was somewhat mitigated.
Nevertheless, the fact remained that Rosa Luxemburg, the revolutionary and the martyr, had expressed strong disapprobation of
certain aspects of the victorious proletarian revolution.

It was, like all Rosa Luxemburg's writings, vivid and impassioned, a plaint inspired by the glaring contrast between glorious
vision and sordid reality. She hails the revolution as the culmination of 'a century of European development', criticizes the Mensheviks for their 'reactionary tactics', and congratulates the
Bolsheviks on having 'solved the famous problem of "winning
a majority of the people" '. This, then, was the 'mass' revolution
of which Rosa had dreamed. But this vision (after all, the

essay was written in prison with limited access to information about what was going on) led to a paradoxical conclusion. If this was really a revolution of the masses, then why all these compromises – on the land question, on the national question – with imperial Germany at Brest-Litovsk? Why the curtailment of the freedom of the press? Why dictatorship and the terror? All these things are passed in review, and Lenin's policies found wanting.

What Rosa Luxemburg was doing was clearly enough to judge the practice of the revolution in the light of the revolutionary ideal. This was a salutary exercise for those committed to the revolutionary cause, but of little relevance to those opposed to the revolution as such. As Mr Nettl justly observes, 'those who are made joyful by criticism of the fundamentals of the Bolshevik revolution would do better to turn elsewhere'. But this would be asking too much of the propagandists. Today this fragmentary essay, which its author never completed or prepared for publication, is far better known, at any rate in the English-speaking world, than any of her finished writings. Yet another edition of the English translation has recently been issued for propagandist purposes, with a polemical introduction, by an American university press.

This sort of thing has, of course, been matched, and to some extent provoked, from the other side. For some years after her death Rosa Luxemburg continued to be honoured in the Soviet Union as a revolutionary leader and a martyr to the cause, an adversary of Lenin, but a respected though misguided adversary, on certain specific questions. But, as the blight of Stalinism settled down on the USSR, and as her writings came to be freely used by hostile propagandists, Rosa came more and more to be identified as one of the great heretics, and her views were assimilated to Trotskyism and Menshevism. The economic analysis of *The Accumulation of Capital*, pointing to the inevitability of the collapse of capitalism when it no longer had 'colonial' areas of the world to exploit, was denounced not only as a derogation from true Marxism but as an endorsement of the 'determinist' aspects of Menshevism. With the collapse of the extremer forms of Stalinism, vituperation of Rosa Luxemburg is no longer in order; and her memory is honoured, though not without mention of her errors, in eastern Germany and in Poland. It would be pleasant to be able to look forward to a propaganda truce on both sides. There is something indecent in the use of Rosa's name and writings as a cold-war missile.

Rosa Luxemburg's most pertinent criticisms turned on two points. Writing under the influence of the acceptance of the Brest-Litovsk treaty, she feared an alliance between Russian Bolshevism and German imperialism; Lenin, she felt, was preparing to sacrifice the interests of the international proletariat, and of the German revolution, to those of the Russian state. The apprehension was, for the moment, unjust and ill-founded, though it might be thought that Rosa Luxemburg showed remarkable prescience of tendencies which revealed themselves later at Rapallo and eventually in the Nazi-Soviet pact of 1939. The other criticism was a return to her strictures of 1904; Lenin had realized a dictatorship not of the majority, but of the minority, imposed by rigid discipline and methods of terror incompatible with the true nature of socialism.

This was the ultimate point on which Rosa Luxemburg took her stand. Unlike Marx and Engels, who never renounced the heritage of the French revolution with its tradition of terror, Rosa Luxemburg believed that the socialist revolution could be achieved only when it was willed by an overwhelming majority of the workers, and that this majority would make the use of violent methods unnecessary. Her humanitarian and idealistic outlook shrank from the violence which she in theory advocated and justified. She bridged this gap – to her own satisfaction – by a fanatical but utopian, almost anarchist, faith in the masses. The 'mass strike' became on her lips a political panacea. Action was more important than organization. Mass action, as the expression of the will of the majority, was the antithesis of dictatorship, though it had equally little to do with liberal or bourgeois democracy.

Rosa was never obliged formally to take a stand as between

Russian Bolsheviks and Mensheviks, whose differences were little understood outside Russia. Temperamentally she certainly leaned towards the Bolsheviks and the doctrine of revolutionary action. But it is easy to see how quickly her idealism was bound to clash with Lenin's hard-headed demands for strict party discipline and an elite of trained revolutionary leaders. The essence of her faith was most clearly and briefly expressed in the programme which she drafted for the German Communist Party.

> The essence of socialist society consists in the fact that the great working mass ceases to be a regimented mass, and itself lives and directs in free conscious self-determination the whole political and economic life. . . .
> The proletarian revolution needs for its purposes no terror, it hates and abominates murder. . . . It is no desperate attempt of a minority to fashion the world after its own ideal, but the action of the great mass of the millions of the people which is called to carry out the mission of history, to transform historical necessity into reality.

How much there was of the utopian in these noble ideals in the Germany of 1918–19 was shown by Rosa Luxemburg's murder just two weeks after they had been formally adopted by the young Communist Party as articles of its programme. The military and police officers who killed Luxemburg and Liebknecht – and not only they, but the hooligans of more than one party who had clamoured for the blood of the Communist leaders – were the forerunners of the thugs who found the final fulfilment of their mission in Hitler's Germany.

IV *The Bolshevik Utopia*

No movement that sets out to change the world can do without its Utopia, its vision of a future which will reward the exertions, and outweigh the sufferings, of the present. Most religions have strongly marked utopian elements; and European civilization has been cradled in the Jewish, the Mohammedan, and especially the Christian, Utopias. The Christian Utopia, though it shared many of the material characteristics of the Jewish and Mohammedan Utopias, had a peculiar quality of its own. It looked forward to the ultimate triumph not of the rich and powerful, but of the poor, humble and weak. It was to be achieved by non-violent means; and the transformation of human nature played an essential part in it. The lion would lie down with the lamb. The adoption of Christianity as the official religion of western civilization has perpetuated and legitimized these utopian elements, though in a much weakened form, in western thought.

With the birth, or re-birth, of a secular civilization after the Renaissance, the concept of Utopia was also secularized. The first secular Utopia, which gave the concept its modern name, dates from the sixteenth century, and had many successors. The next landmark in the history of Utopia was the Enlightenment. None of the major Enlightenment thinkers was, strictly speaking, a utopian; the construction of Utopias was left to minor figures like Mably and Morelly. But Rousseau had conspicuous utopian traits; Turgot wrote a *Tableau philosophique des progrès successifs de l'esprit humain*; and Condorcet, of the second generation of the Enlightenment, was an out-and-out Utopian, who believed in 'the infinite perfection of our species' as 'a general law of nature', and, after himself falling a victim to the revolution, was afterwards accepted as one of its principal ideologues. What emerged from all this turmoil of thought was a marriage between Utopia and the Cult of Reason. The progress of the human spirit was assured through the ever-increasing cultivation and application of reason. Utopia meant the triumph of rational man.

Romanticism, though it reacted against the empirical rationalism of the Enlightenment, added its quota of encouragement and inspiration to utopian visions of the liberation of man from a constricting environment. The first half of the nineteenth century, and especially the years after 1830, was the golden age of utopianism, culminating in the creation not only of the most fanciful and elaborate literary Utopias, but of ideal communities whose members lived and worked together in perfect harmony and pre-figured the universal society of the future. Marx grew up in this atmosphere. The utopian tradition tended to flow in two divergent channels. The first stream – that of Rousseau, the Jacobins, Fourier, Owen – saw progress primarily in moral terms, in the triumph of virtue and the re-shaping of human nature. The other stream – Turgot, Condorcet, Saint-Simon – saw progress primarily in economic and technical terms, in the rise of productivity and the extension of scientific knowledge. Marx, perhaps unconsciously, synthesized these two approaches to the advance of civilization. The combination in him of the prophetic moralist and the cool scientist has often been remarked, and later led to differences of interpretation (though the difference here is not identical) between 'voluntarist' and 'determinist' schools of Marxism. Marx's attitude to Utopia was ambivalent. The *Communist Manifesto*, in a section entitled 'Critical-Utopian Socialism and Communism', gave qualified praise to the 'practical proposals' of the school, most of which eventually found their way into Marx's own programme: 'Abolition of the distinction between town and country, of the family, of the carrying on of industries for the account of private individuals, and of the wage-system,

the proclamation of social harmony, the conversion of the functions of the state into a mere superintendence of production.'
What Marx condemned in utopian socialism was its unhistorical character. It took no account of the class struggle, and its expositors placed themselves 'in opposition to the historical development of the proletariat'. Marx contrasted utopianism with his own historical approach; and, as time went on, he came to insist more and more emphatically on the scientific character of his work. His task was to confirm and demonstrate, by scientific reasoning, the prediction of the *Communist Manifesto* that the downfall of the bourgeoisie and the victory of the proletariat were 'equally inevitable'. 'In Marx', observed Lenin in *State and Revolution*, 'there is no trace of any attempt to construct Utopias, to guess in the void about what cannot be known.'

The failures and disillusionments which followed the revolutions of 1848 created a climate unpropitious to Utopias. The age of *Realpolitik* had set in; even rising socialist parties began to think in terms of what was practically possible rather than of what was ideally desirable. Utopia was not indeed in total eclipse. The sudden flare-up of the Paris commune, with its markedly utopian inspiration, was not wholly extinguished by official repression and by the weight of respectable opinion. Though Marx in his later years was increasingly reluctant to speculate about the future, Engels kept alive the utopian elements in the original doctrine. A synthesis between Utopia and science was not peculiar to Marxism. The liberal doctrine of progress reached the height of its popularity in the second half of the nineteenth century. Like Marx in his later years, it shied away from visionary predictions. But its essence was compounded of the same two elements of Utopia and science.

Moreover, such discrediting of Utopia as occurred in these years in the west did not extend to eastern Europe, where a regime repressive of any critical opinion or practical public activity left the way open for imaginative excursions in the realm of political idealism. The most famous utopian work of this period, Chernyshevsky's novel, *What is to be Done?*, served as a bible for two generations of Russian radicals and revolutionaries. The Russian anarchists and narodniks were steeped in utopian thought; Tolstoy's beliefs and writings were deeply marked by it. This was the atmosphere in which Marxism began to permeate and influence Russian revolutionary doctrine, and in which Lenin grew up. The victory of the revolution and its sequel have given currency to a picture of Lenin as the hard-headed politician and ruthless organizer. But even the early essay in which Lenin first presented himself in this character – *What is to be Done?*, named after Chernyshevsky's novel – contained a rarely quoted passage on 'the need to dream'. Lenin covered himself with a long quotation from the nihilist Pisarev:

> My dream may catch up with a natural course of events, or it may go completely astray in a direction where the natural course of events can never arrive. In the first case the dream cannot do any kind of harm; it may even support and strengthen the energy of the man in his work. . . . If man were completely deprived of the capacity to dream in this way, if he could not from time to time run ahead, and through his imagination see, in the whole and complete picture, the creation which is just beginning to shape itself in his hands, then I really cannot conceive what driving force could compel a man to undertake and to bring to a conclusion extensive and exhausting labours in art, in science, and in practical life.

And Lenin lamented that there were too few such dreams 'in our movement', and too many people who prided themselves on their sobriety and their ' "nearness" to the "concrete" '.

Lenin the utopian dreamer is therefore a part of the man. The utopian aspirations of early Bolshevism were an essential part of it, and cannot be neglected. For the idealization of simple untutored human nature, which since Rousseau had been the stock in trade of utopians, Marxists substituted the idealization of the proletariat. When the brutal realities of the First World War stimulated utopian speculation everywhere, and western liberals preached the brotherhood of man to be attained through a league of nations, and Wilson put his faith in the right judgement of plain men throughout the world, Lenin in *State and Revolution*, the most utopian of all his writings, expounded his vision of a society in which, after the destruction of the bourgeois state and the ending of class antagonisms, the coercive functions of the state would wither away, and the necessary and much simplified functions of administration and of the ordering of the economy would be performed by ordinary workers, acting in rotation: 'People will gradually *become accustomed* to the observance of elementary rules of living together – rules known for centuries and repeated for thousands of years in all codes of behaviour – to their observance without force, without compulsion, without subordination, *without that special apparatus* for compulsion which is called the state.' This work was written in the summer of 1917 while Lenin was waiting for conditions to ripen for the seizure of power by the Bolsheviks, and published in the spring of 1918 when the Bolshevik regime had begun to establish itself.

The eighth party congress, held in March 1919 at the height of the civil war and just after the congress which founded the Communist International, changed the name of the party from Russian Social-Democratic Workers' Party to Russian Communist Party (Bolsheviks), and issued a new party programme. This rehearsed the sections of the old programme of 1903 which analysed the causes of the impending downfall of capitalism and victory of the proletariat, celebrated the achievement of the October revolution of 1917, and defined the principal goals and tasks, long-term and short-term, of the revolutionary regime. A few months later two young party intellectuals, Nikolai Bukharin and Evgenii Preobrazhensky, wrote under the title *The ABC of Communism* a commentary on the programme, which they described in the preface as 'an elementary textbook of communist knowledge'. For ten years it was constantly reprinted and translated, circulating widely in many countries as an authoritative exposition of the 'aims and tasks' of communism. It has not

been reprinted in the Soviet Union since the end of the 1920s
when both its authors had fallen into political disgrace.

The ABC of Communism provides an unrivalled key to the
purposes and policies of communism as they were conceived in
the first years of the regime. Divided into a 'theoretical' part
which analyses the decline and fall of capitalism leading up to
the communist revolution, and a 'practical' part dealing with the
dictatorship of the proletariat and the creation of the communist
order, it is a striking amalgam of the practical with the utopian;
and a review of the successes and failures registered in the realization of this programme offers a broad conspectus of the achievements of the revolution.

The October revolution meant, in terms of Marxist prophecy,
the destruction of the existing Russian state order, and its replacement by the dictatorship of the proletariat. It was anomalous
that the defeated regime could not in any strict sense be called
unconditionally bourgeois or capitalist, and that the revolution
which overthrew it was itself in a transitional stage, and dis-
charged bourgeois as well as socialist functions. But in 1919,
when the new party programme was adopted and *The ABC of
Communism* appeared, it was no longer fashionable to dwell on
these anomalies, though the Russian revolution was still confidently regarded as the prelude to a more far-reaching European
or world-wide revolution. What was clear was that the Soviet
Government, which embodied the dictatorship of the proletariat,
was class government. It was officially called a 'Workers' and
Peasants' Government'; Lenin on one occasion, invoking the
precedent of the Paris commune, called it 'the state of the
commune'. Its aim was to complete the destruction of the former
state machine, and to eliminate the bourgeoisie. Once this had
been achieved, class antagonisms would have disappeared; and,
since every state was the expression and instrument of class
conflict, the new state, i.e. the dictatorship of the proletariat,
would itself 'ripen into communism, dying away together with
the state organization of society'.[1]

[1] Bukharin, *Ekonomika Perekhodnogo Perioda*, i 110.

The withering away of the state, the most conspicuously utopian element in Marxist doctrine, must be seen in the light of the familiar nineteenth-century dichotomy of society and state. Adam Smith had the vision of a society of producers and traders in which the state performed certain limited functions. Hegel, though his conclusion was different, built up his political system on the antithesis between civil society and state power. Marx not only accepted the current opposition of society to the state, but reinforced it by a special view of the relation between them, which reflected more of the influence of Smith than of Hegel. Marx clearly established the distinction implicit in Adam Smith, though not drawn by him, between economics and politics, giving priority to the former. Civil society, wrote Marx, 'embraces the whole material intercourse of individuals within a definite stage of the development of productive forces'. The state was the form in which 'the rule of a definite social class . . . has its *practical*-idealistic expression'.[1] Civil society became an economic, the state a political, conception.

These views led to a widespread tendency of nineteenth-century western political thought to idealize society and to treat the state as something inherently evil. Society consisted of men of good will working freely together for the common good; the state was the instrument or symbol of compulsion imposed on them from above. This attitude found its logical and extreme expression in anarchism. But enlightened thinkers looked forward to an extension of the voluntary ordering of affairs characteristic of society, and to the disappearance of the coercive functions of the state. Saint-Simon coined a phrase which enjoyed a long reign of popularity when he foretold that 'the administration of things' would replace 'the government of men'. Politics would be dissolved into economics. Marx found this view congenial, and quickly adapted it to his own analysis of the nature of the state. When the workers came to power, there would, he wrote in an early work, 'no longer be political power properly so called, since political power is precisely the official embodiment of the antago-

[1] Marx and Engels, *The German Ideology*, 48, 85.

nism in civil society'.[1] Marx, however, using the dialectical term
Aufhebung, spoke of the state being 'superseded' or 'transcended'.
He thus adopted the Hegelian dichotomy of 'civil society' and
'state', but reversed the Hegelian conclusion. The ultimate synthesis would be achieved, and the opposition between society and
state resolved, not through the dissolution of civil society in the
state, but by the dissolution of the state in society as a whole.
Engels insisted that 'when the state becomes in reality the representative of the whole society, it renders itself superfluous'; and
it was Engels who, rashly invoking the biological metaphor of
'withering' or 'dying', proclaimed that 'as soon as there is no
longer any social class to be held in subjection, the state *dies
away*'.

In the twenty years which separated the death of Engels from
the First World War, the growth of state power everywhere, and
the increasing inclination of western socialist parties to rely on the
use of state machinery to achieve their ends, discouraged any talk
of the withering away of the state. The outbreak of war, while it
affirmed the readiness of a majority of western socialists to co-
operate with their national states, provoked the converse reaction
among those socialists who were opposed to the war. The point in
Bukharin's war-time diatribes against the 'national state' which
aroused Lenin's disapproval was not his hostility to existing states,
but his assumption that the machinery of the state would become
superfluous, and disappear, immediately on the seizure of power
by the workers. Lenin, in *State and Revolution*, more cautiously
explained that it was the bourgeois state which would be destroyed
by the proletarian revolution; it was the proletarian state which
would gradually die away. But he concluded that, even under
capitalism, technical innovations (factories, railways, posts and
telegraphs) had created a situation in which 'the vast majority
of the functions of the old "state government" have been simplified, and can be reduced to simple operations of registration,
record and verification'. Lenin at this time placed considerably

[1] *Marx-Engels Gesamtausgabe* (1932) I, vi 227; the words occur in the
polemic against Proudhon, *La Misère de la philosophie*, written in 1847.

greater emphasis on the eventual disappearance of the state than
on the temporary necessity to maintain and reinforce it through
the dictatorship of the proletariat.

After the revolution, when the need for order, organization
and discipline became paramount, this emphasis was reversed.
When the new party programme was adopted in March 1919,
insistence on the class character of the proletarian dictatorship
as an instrument for 'crushing the resistance of the exploiters',
and on the multifarious tasks to be performed by the Soviet state,
already eclipsed the inconspicuous references to the eventual
disappearance of state power; and Bukharin in *The ABC of
Communism* reflected that it was only 'in proportion as there
comes a speedier end to the attempts made by the exploiters to
overthrow communism' that 'the proletarian state will gradually
die out, and will undergo transformation into a stateless communist society'. The dictatorship of the proletariat retained 'a
formal resemblance' to the dictatorship of the bourgeoisie: it was
'state capitalism *in reverse, its dialectical transformation into its
own opposite*'.[1] The vision, however, remained. *The ABC of
Communism* insisted that 'every member of a Soviet should
play some definite part in the work of state administration',
that all functions should be exercised in rotation, and that 'by
degrees the entire working population shall be induced to participate in state administration'. A year later, in *The Theory of
Historical Materialism*, Bukharin continued to assert that, in the
future communist society, 'there will be *absolutely* no external
(legal) regulation', since 'men of the new mould, fully conscious
and reared in the spirit of working solidarity, will need no
external incentives'.[2] In succeeding years the doctrine of the
withering away of the state was sparingly invoked in communist
literature; and references to it were customarily balanced by the
assertion that the isolation of the USSR in a hostile capitalist
world made a strong state power more, not less, necessary. It is
correct that periods of emergency and crisis appear to lead to an

[1] Bukharin, *Ekonomika Perekhodnogo Perioda*, i 63–4.
[2] N. Bukharin, *Teoriya Istoricheskogo Materializma* (1921) 21.

inflation of state power. But deeper influences have also been at work. The world-wide accretion in the scope and effectiveness of state authority, which has weakened or effaced the clear nine-teenth-century dichotomy of state and society, and stultified nineteenth-century utopian visions of the withering away of the state, seems to be due primarily to dynamic changes in the processes of production.

* * *

Belief in the eventual atrophy of the political authority of the state in no way implied belief in the extinction of economic authority exercised by society for the purpose of maintaining and expanding production. While 'the merely repressive organs of the old governmental power' had to be destroyed, wrote Marx in *The Civil War in France* after the experience of the Paris Commune, 'its legitimate functions' were to be restored to 'the responsible agents of society'. The eighteenth-century Physio-crats and, after them, the classical economists created an economic science revolving round the concept of productivity; and Marx, who stood on their shoulders, treated production through labour as the specifically human activity. The industrial revolution made increased production the symbol and the driving-force for pro-gress. The Russian party programme of March 1919 was cate-gorical on this point: 'It is an essential part of the economic policy of the Soviet power to secure a universal increase in the productive forces of the country. . . . All other considerations must be subordinated to one practical aim – a rapid increase, by all available means, in the quantity of goods urgently needed by the population.' Where, however, production occupied this cen-tral place in society, the organization of production could not be altogether neglected; and this need grew with the increasing scale and complexity of industry. Marx, in the third volume of *Capital*, noted that 'all labour in which many individuals co-operate necessarily requires a commanding will to co-ordinate and unify the process'. Engels, in repeating the famous Saint-Simonian formula, identified 'the administration of things' with 'the direction of the processes of production'. Elsewhere he spoke of society 'openly and directly taking possession of the productive forces'. In an article which originally appeared in Italian in 1874, though it was not published in German till 1913, he observed the growing complication of the processes of production, and concluded: 'The automatic machinery of a big factory is much more despotic than the small capitalists who employ workers have ever been. . . . Wanting to abolish authority in large-scale industry is tantamount to wanting to abolish industry itself.' Lenin quoted this passage in *State and Revolution*, the very work in which he proclaimed the doctrine of the withering away of the state.

Belief in the disappearance of the state apparatus was thus rendered plausible by belief that society would find other ways to organize and control the economic process independently of it. Lenin, in the well-known article 'Will the Bolsheviks Retain State Power?' written in September 1917, argued that the state machinery of production, unlike the machinery of coercion, 'should not be broken up' but should be 'wrested from the control of the capitalists' and 'subordinated to proletarian Soviets'. *The ABC of Communism* made it clear that the superseding of the state by society rested on the assumption that ownership and control of the means of production 'is not the privilege of a class, but of all the persons who make up the society'. It did not mean the end of all organization; on the contrary, 'communist society is organized throughout'. This process began even under the temporary dictatorship of the proletariat. 'The essential characteristic of the proletarian state', wrote Preobrazhensky in one of the chapters for which he was responsible, 'is its gradual transformation from an unproductive organization to become an organization for the administration of economic life.'

The instrument through which society would free itself 'from the anarchy of production, from competition between individual entrepreneurs, from wars and crises' was planning. The organization of the economy 'presupposes a general plan of production'. In the future communist society, when the state would no longer exist, 'the main direction will be entrusted to various kinds of bookkeeping offices or statistical bureaux' where 'account will be kept of production and all its needs'. In the second or 'practical' part of *The ABC of Communism*, where the role of the 'Soviet state' in the transitional period is fully recognized, one of '*the fundamental tasks of the Soviet power*' is defined as '*that of uniting all the economic activities of the country in accordance with a general plan of direction by the state*'.

The sections of *The ABC of Communism* dealing with the expansion of production under communism, though some of the arguments invoked in them[1] are one-sided and unrealistic, are those which have best withstood the test of time. 'The basis of communist society must be the social ownership of the means of production and exchange.' 'As soon as victory has been achieved, and as soon as all our wounds have been healed, the communist society will rapidly develop the forces of production. . . . The communist method of production will signify an enormous development of productive forces.' 'The foundation of our whole policy must be the widest possible development of productivity.' The problems involved in the expansion of production – how to increase material means of production and the labour force, how to organize relations between different branches of production, how to improve the quality of work through better labour discipline, and how to apply science to production and recruit skilled experts – are fairly stated, and the difficulties not ignored. Finally non-material goals are also stressed. 'The working day will grow continually shorter, and people will be to an increasing extent freed from the chains imposed on them by nature. As soon as man is enabled to spend less time upon feeding and clothing himself, he will be able to devote more time to the work of mental development. . . . Men and women will for the first time be able to lead a life worthy of

[1] The principal arguments are that communism will liberate for productive purposes the energies and resources now absorbed in the class struggle, or wasted in 'competition, crises and wars'; will profit by the economies of large-scale production; and will eliminate the parasitical elements in capitalist society and employ them in productive labour.

thinking human beings instead of a life worthy of brute beasts.'

In the first fifty years after the revolution, the population of the USSR, in spite of the ravages of two world wars, a civil war, and two serious famines, rose from 140 millions to over 200 millions. This increase was accompanied by an enormous growth of urban population (15 per cent of total population in towns in 1914, nearly 60 per cent in 1967), and a change-over from a high proportion of illiteracy or semi-literacy to total literacy and a widely diffused standard of secondary and higher education; and the USSR has become the second industrial nation in the world, with pre-eminence in many of the most advanced and sophisticated processes of production. These phenomenal achievements show that Bukharin's optimistic and partly utopian prognostications were not wholly wide of the mark. It is sometimes argued that the industrial development of the USSR, which had begun before the revolution, had nothing to do with the communist regime. But this argument is difficult to reconcile with the fact that many procedures first preached by the Bolsheviks and emphatically repudiated elsewhere – the nationalization of major industries, planned economy, the rejection of the superior authority of finance, the integration of the trade unions into the control of economic policies – were later adopted, sometimes in covert and roundabout ways, in many western countries. It may still be said that what has happened in these respects, in the USSR and elsewhere, has been the product of deep-seated trends due primarily to changing industrial technology and not to any revolutionary ideology. Even so, it seems fair to recognize that the USSR, thanks to the impetus of the revolution and to an ideology more amenable to the needs of modern technological development than the *laissez-faire* liberalism in which western capitalism was nurtured, has placed itself in the van of contemporary industrial progress.

Agriculture and the peasantry receive relatively little attention in *The ABC of Communism*. The support of the peasant was a necessary condition of the success of the revolution, and of its victory in the civil war. Yet the peasantry was not a single class;

and the 'middle peasant', who formed the majority, 'see-saws between the proletariat and the bourgeoisie'. The chapter on agriculture written by Preobrazhensky rehearsed the well-known and conclusive arguments in favour of large-scale cultivation. But the modest projects designed to promote it – Soviet farms, communes and artels, agricultural co-operatives – were plainly inadequate to counteract the drive for the equal re-partition of the land in small peasant holdings which followed the revolution. State subsidies and propaganda were the only methods suggested to foster large-scale agriculture. The words 'it is absolutely clear that forcible expropriation is here quite inadmissible' occurred in the context of petty industrial craftsmen and artisans. But they were equally applicable to the small-scale peasant producer. Before 1929 no party authority was prepared to contemplate the forced expropriation and collectivization of the peasant. The problem of the capital accumulation necessary to finance an expanding industry, and of the peasantry as the main source of such accumulation, which was to preoccupy Preobrazhensky in his major work and to become the central axis of economic policy, finds as yet no echo in *The ABC of Communism*.

*   *   *

The party programme, and every vision of the communist society of the future, turns on the role of the proletariat. Labour is the source of production and therefore, in Marxist doctrine, of all value; it is the essential human activity. In the capitalist world the typical suppliers of labour power are the factory proletariat. The proletariat under capitalism becomes the revolutionary class. By rising in revolt, it overthrows the ruling bourgeoisie and thus eliminates itself, i.e. ceases to be a proletariat, leading mankind into the Utopia of the classless society in which there will be no more exploitation of man by man. This social transformation implies a transformation of man himself. As Marx put it in 1850,

'We say to the workers: You will have to live through 20, 30, 50 years of civil wars and battles, not only in order to transform the social system, but in order also to transform yourselves and to become capable of exercising political supremacy.' 'Within a few decades', proclaims *The ABC of Communism*, 'there will be quite a new world, with new people and new customs.' This vision inspired countless pronouncements and publications of more than one generation of Russian revolutionaries.

In the thinking of Lenin and of every Bolshevik, the October revolution was a proletarian revolution (the active part in executing the *coup* in Petrograd was played by organized factory workers), and the Soviet form of government set up by it was the dictatorship of the proletariat envisaged by Marx as a transitional stage to the eventual classless and stateless society. The proletariat not only constituted the government; it also became the owner of the means of production. Among the means of production thus nationalized the land occupied an important place. The theoretical difficulty involved in the still overwhelming predominance of agriculture in the Russian economy was met by the recognition of the peasant as a sort of junior partner with the worker in the regime, which was officially styled a 'Workers' and Peasants' Government'. The potential clash of interests between proletariat and peasantry came into the open only much later, and finds no reflection in the pages of *The ABC of Communism*; in 1919 worker and peasant were still firmly united by a common interest in consolidating the victory of the revolution. But another problem was already beginning to rear its head: how to reconcile the dual function of the worker as ruler and ruled, as sovereign and subject of the proletarian dictatorship. Had the transitional period been brief – and during the first months and years the Bolshevik leaders confidently looked for a European revolution to bring it to an end – the problem might have been evaded or postponed. But, as the period of the proletarian dictatorship and the slow transition to communism prolonged itself indefinitely, the issue of relations between the worker and the regime became in practice increasingly acute.

The issue was constantly raised by critics of the regime in terms of the rights of the individual – and especially of the rights to liberty and equality proclaimed by the French revolution. The Marxist critique challenged this conception in two respects. In the first place, these rights were conceived as being exclusively legal and political – the sense in which the phrase 'civil rights' was commonly used. But for a vast majority of people what was decisive for their way of life was economic status. In practice only the economically independent enjoyed legal and political rights (in Marx's day political rights were, even formally, still restricted to them in most western countries), and used these rights to assert and maintain their economic independence; for the economically dependent the enjoyment of civil rights remained ineffective and meaningless. Secondly, the conception of the rights of the individual had been valid and important in the period of the French revolution, when it had been necessary to destroy a society based on legally entrenched and privileged 'orders', and when the individual entrepreneur and worker were still familiar figures on the economic scene. But its validity was gradually sapped during a century which, while loudly trumpeting the rights of the individual, witnessed his progressive reabsorption into more and more powerful groups of a new kind, so that by the beginning of the twentieth century the individual producer had become a rare and peripheral phenomenon, and the ordinary individual could as a rule exercise his rights, and even his chosen occupation, only by joining the appropriate group and subscribing to its written or unwritten rules and conventions. These developments once more lent plausibility to the assumption that the individual could achieve self-fulfilment only through society, not against society. In Russia, which had never experienced on any significant scale the period of the individual producer, the doctrine of individual rights had had few adherents, even among revolutionaries. The Marxist critique of western theory and practice found here a ready response. It was taken so much for granted by the authors of *The ABC of Communism* that they conduct the argument in a rather perfunctory way, and with little consciousness of the case that can be brought against it.

The argument proceeds on the assumption of the proletariat as a collective entity. The notion of a potential individual worker with interests or ambitions opposed to those of the majority of workers is not so much dismissed as ignored. The deduction follows that once the capitalist has been expropriated, and the means of production transferred to the proletarian state, 'the whole basis of exploitation is destroyed'. The reasoning is clear: 'The proletarian state cannot exploit the proletariat, for the simple reason that it is itself an organization of the proletariat. A man cannot climb upon his own back. The proletariat cannot exploit its own self.' The same consideration applies to discipline in factories:

> Labour discipline must be based upon the feeling and *the consciousness that every worker is responsible to his class*, upon the consciousness that slackness and carelessness are treason to the common cause of the workers. . . . The workers no longer work for capitalists, usurers and bankers; they work for themselves. . . . Since all the comrades know that a decline in the productivity of labour will involve the ruin of the whole working class, . . . they must all supervise with a proprietary eye the common task of utilizing the life-giving energies of nature.

The worker is required to render to the workers' state and its organs the same loyalty as is demanded from the worker in capitalist countries to the trade union.[1] The worker who seeks to act in his own interest independently of the group, and in opposition to it, is a blackleg, and is deservedly excluded from the community of workers. It is significant that the trade-union analogy was often applied in party controversy and dissidents branded as blacklegs and 'strike-breakers'.

[1] Bukharin later (*Ekonomika Perekhodnogo Perioda*, i 114–15) pointed out that, even in capitalist countries, the trade unions, by abolishing competition between workers and insisting on the closed shop, had in part abrogated 'freedom of labour' in the bourgeois sense, which meant encouragement of strike-breakers.

The argument was reinforced by a point frequently made by Bukharin at this time – the existence of strata or layers within the proletariat itself. In theoretical analysis classes could be treated as entities and minor differences within them ignored. But this was not the real situation. In capitalist society a 'labour aristocracy' of privileged workers arose within the working class. The Russian proletariat comprised not only a hard core of seasoned factory workers, but large numbers of former peasants newly recruited into factory work and still retaining more or less active associations with the countryside, as well as a handful of formerly independent artisans and craftsmen, and agricultural labourers often still holding small plots of land and barely distinguishable from poor peasants. To train these people as factory workers, and to inculcate in them a proletarian class consciousness, was a task requiring labour, patience and stern discipline. This placed an immense responsibility on the vanguard of the proletariat, identified in practice with the party: 'Until the vanguard of the workers learn to organize tens of millions', said Lenin in April 1918, 'they are not yet socialists and not creators of the socialist society.' From this disparate and variegated composition of the proletariat Bukharin deduced the paradoxical need for 'compulsory discipline', which he sometimes called '*compulsory self-discipline*', of the workers under the dictatorship of the proletariat.[1]

In this scheme of things the trade unions had an important role to play. The party, the Soviets and the trade unions were all different organizations of the proletariat; in the revolution they had 'marched side by side against the capitalist social order'. In the new order created by the revolution the Soviets were the 'instruments of state power'; the trade unions (and the co-operatives) were to 'develop in such a way that they will be transformed into economic departments and instruments of the state authority'. Bukharin looked forward to the time when '*the whole of economic life, from the bottom to the top, shall constitute a unity which is effectively controlled by the industrial unions*'. The

[1] The best statement of this argument is in Bukharin, *Ekonomika Perekhodnogo Perioda*, i 141–3.

main task of the unions as organs of economic policy was to raise productivity by enlisting the co-operation of the workers in the process of production. The identical status of party, Soviets and trade unions as organs of the proletariat rendered heretical any claim to independence on the part of the unions; it also ruled out any notion of a legitimate interest of individual workers differing from that of the union as a whole or, consequently, from that of party or state organs. Trotsky at a trade-union congress in 1920 put the issue in a few of those blunt and trenchant phrases which often gave offence:

> We know slave-labour, we know serf-labour, we know the compulsory, regimented labour of the mediaeval guilds, we have known the hired wage-labour which the bourgeoisie calls 'free'. We are now advancing towards a type of labour socially regulated on the basis of an economic plan which is obligatory for the whole country, i.e. compulsory for every worker. . . . We know that all labour is socially compulsory labour. Man must work in order not to die. He does not want to work. But the social organization compels and whips him in that direction.[1]

The total identification of the interests of the individual with those of the group, and recognition of party, government and trade unions as different organs of the same constituent body, the proletariat, made any discussion of individual liberty in western terms inapplicable. Western liberalism conceived the individual as having rights against the state; its attitude to the rights of individuals against other collective entities was governed by the assumption that membership by the individual of such groups was voluntary and contractual, and that any difference between individual and group would normally be resolved by exercise of the right, enjoyed equally by both sides, to terminate the membership. Though the rights of the individual against the state have been partially eroded over a number of years, and though the assumption of voluntary membership of some major groups, and notably of the trade unions, has long been unrealistic, liberal theory has not been revised. Soviet theorists assume that

[1] *Tretii Vserossiiskii S"ezd Professional'nykh Soyuzov* (1920) i 28.

effective political or economic action can proceed only from
groups, and that, for groups to be politically or economically
effective, they must be able to count on the loyalty and obedience
of the members to collective decisions. The individual worker
enjoys no rights against the workers' state or the workers' trade
union other than the right to participate in its activities. When
The ABC of Communism speaks of freedom (which is not very
often) it is concerned either to expose the 'fictitious' freedom
enjoyed by the workers under capitalism or to explain that the
freedom achieved under the dictatorship of the proletariat is not
freedom for all but freedom for the proletariat as an entity. The
notion that this implies freedom for every individual worker is
as unrealistic as the assumption of the rights of the individual
worker against his trade union. Bukharin did not, in *The ABC
of Communism*, dwell in detail – though it is implied throughout –
on the extent to which this conception of freedom pre-supposes
both a new type of society and a new type of man. This he did in
The Theory of Historical Materialism published in the following
year. Here he explained at length that the removal of all contradictions in society brings about a unity between the individual
will and 'the collectively organized will'.[1] In *The Economics of
the Transitional Period* he drew the conclusion still more clearly:
'In communist society there will be absolute freedom of the
"personality"; any kind of external regulation of relations between men will be absent, and self-activity without compulsion
will therefore exist.'[2] The cult of liberty ends in this vision of
self-motivated and self-disciplined anarchy.

The concept of equality has even deeper roots in Marxist
thought, and a more conspicuous place in the Marxist Utopia,
than the concept of liberty. This followed an ancient tradition.
The Stoics postulated perfect equality in a state of nature; and
the early Christian fathers attributed inequalities between human
beings to the Fall. Marx in the first volume of *Capital* started,
in true Hegelian vein, from an abstract human labour which

[1] Bukharin, *Teoriya Istoricheskogo Materializma*, 38–9.
[2] Bukharin, *Ekonomika Perekhodnogo Perioda*, i 144.

was by definition equal and undifferentiated. Not concerning himself with pre-capitalist forms of inequality, he diagnosed inequality in the contemporary world as a symptom and consequence of the division of labour imposed by capitalism.[1] This made labour a class attribute and was, in particular, responsible for an unnatural divorce between intellectual and manual work: 'As in the natural body, head and hand wait on each other, so the labour process unites the labour of the hand with that of the head. Later on, they part company and even become deadly foes.' In the Paris Commune, Marx noted in *The Civil War in France*, public service of all kinds, from top to bottom, was performed *for a worker's wage*. Marx, in common with many other nineteenth-century thinkers from Saint-Simon onwards, believed that the growth of large-scale machine industry, by simplifying the processes of production, would diminish the need for specialization, and mitigate the evils of the division of labour: ' "Let the cobbler stick to his last" (a gem of handicraft wisdom) became an utter absurdity from the moment when a watchmaker, Watt, invented the steam engine; a barber, Arkwright, the throstle; and a working jeweller, Fulton, the steamship.' The 'detail worker' produced by the division of labour would be replaced by 'an individual with an all-round development' ('ein total entwickeltes Individuum'). What this meant in the context of the communist Utopia was described in further flight of fancy.

In communist society, where nobody has an exclusive sphere of activity, but each can become accomplished in any branch he wishes, society regulates the general production, and thus makes it possible for me to do one thing today and another tomorrow, to hunt in the morning, fish in the afternoon, rear cattle in the evening, criticize after dinner, just as I have a mind, without ever becoming hunter, fisherman, shepherd or critic.[2]

---

[1] Engels in an eloquent passage of the *Dialectics of Nature* declared that the great men of the Renaissance were 'not yet in thrall to the division of labour'.

[2] Marx and Engels, *The German Ideology*, 22, 67. This was an early work; but towards the end of his life, in the *Critique of the Gotha Programme*, Marx still looked forward to the disappearance under communism of the distinction between intellectual and manual work.

While it may be assumed that Marx, in this rather light-hearted passage, was more concerned to assert the right to choose one's occupation, and the abolition of social distinctions between occupations ('productive labour ceases to be a class attribute'), than the right to change one's occupation daily or hourly at will, it was echoed in Lenin's vision of the periodical performance of the tasks of administration by workers, and was paraphrased in an undiluted form in *The ABC of Communism*:

> Under communism people receive a many-sided culture, and find themselves at home in many branches of production: today I work in an administrative capacity, I reckon up how many felt boots or how many French rolls must be produced in the following month; tomorrow I shall be working in a soap-factory, next month perhaps in a steam-laundry, the month after in an electric power station. This will be possible when all members of society have been suitably educated.

In particular, through the organization of the trade unions, 'the two great divisions of those who labour, the mental workers and the manual workers, kept asunder by capitalism, will at length be reunited'. Nobody at this time felt it necessary to ask the question which, little more than ten years later, tormented Gramsci as he reflected and wrote in one of Mussolini's prisons: 'Does one start from the premise of a perpetual division of the human race [into rulers and ruled], or does one believe that this is only an historical fact answering to certain conditions?' Technological developments had moved in a different direction from that foreseen by Marx, Lenin and Bukharin, in the direction of greater specialization and therefore greater differentiation: 'In a sense it can be said that the division is a product of the division of labour, that it is a technical fact.' The technical necessity for leadership provoked the melancholy reflection that it was 'difficult to rid the leaders of dictatorial habits' and 'difficult to extirpate the criminal habit of neglecting to avoid useless sacrifices'.[1] This problem was to enter only at a later stage into Soviet consciousness.

[1] A. Gramsci, *The Modern Prince* (Engl. transl. 1957) 143–4.

When *The ABC of Communism* was written, the Soviet regime had been in power for nearly two years and a practical problem of equality had arisen in relation to the remuneration of labour. It proved impossible in practice (the attempt was never seriously made) to break down the traditional wage differentials between skilled and unskilled labour, or between different industries. Still more embarrassingly, it proved impossible to deny far higher rates of pay to former Tsarist officers and engineers employed in responsible posts in the Red Army and in industry.[1] The party programme of March 1919, while identifying 'equal remuneration for all labour' with 'the complete establishment of communism', conceded that 'the Soviet power cannot endeavour to effect the full realization of this equality at the present moment'; and *The ABC of Communism* followed the same cautious line. Throughout the 1920s the belief that inequalities in wages would gradually disappear continued to prevail; Preobrazhensky emphatically asserted in 1924 that a system of differential wages 'has nothing, and can have nothing, in common with socialism'.[2] The trade unions agitated spasmodically against the high salaries paid to specialists, and made attempts to pull up the wages of low-paid workers to higher levels. But the demand for more and more experts as industrial processes became more complex, and the need for incentives to stimulate the worker's productivity, defeated any widespread move towards equalization. When Stalin in 1931 flat-footedly came out in favour of wage differentials, and denounced 'equalization' or 'levelling' as a bourgeois prejudice, he shocked many party consciences, but removed the last official inhibitions about such a policy. While the application of modern advanced technology to industry has enormously increased the numbers and the proportion of technically qualified and highly-trained workers in industry, it has probably widened rather than diminished the gap between top-ranking experts and managers and the rank and

[1] Bukharin in *Ekonomika Perekhodnogo Perioda*, i 65–9, works hard to explain away the anomalous social structure in which, under the dictatorship of the proletariat, Tsarist officers and bourgeois specialists were employed to issue orders to workers.   [2] E. Preobrazhensky, *Novaya Ekonomika* (1926) 176.

file of skilled technicians, and between the qualified technicians and the large number of unskilled or semi-skilled workers still required by society to discharge more menial tasks. The future of equality everywhere in modern industrial society presents a puzzling problem. What may perhaps be said is that in the USSR the Utopia of equal remuneration has retained more vitality than the Utopia of individual liberty, and still inhibits the growth of the more extreme and conspicuous forms of inequality.

Bukharin's personal standpoint on the national question adds a special interest to the chapter of *The ABC of Communism* on 'Communism and the Problem of Nationality'. The chapter was written by Preobrazhensky, whose views appear, however, to have coincided with those of Bukharin. It opens with a disquisition on the artificiality of the barriers to the unity of mankind set up by national divisions and national enmities, and calls on the workers of all countries to recognize one another as 'brothers in oppression and slavery' and to join hands in 'one world-wide league for the struggle with the capitalists': 'Workers of all countries, unite' had always been the essence of the communist creed. Unity was necessary from economic as well as from political considerations. 'If national prejudice and national greed oppose the internationalization of industry and agriculture, away with them, wherever they may show themselves and under whatever colours they may sail!' The oppression of subject nationalities was a legacy from 'the brutal national quarrels of the feudal and capitalist epochs'. Tsarist oppression of Poles, Ukrainians and Jews, as well as of such backward nations as the Tunguses, Kalmucks and Buryats, is cited side by side with the similar sins of the German and the English bourgeoisie. 'A voluntary federative league' is offered as a half-way house to complete unity. But such a league will prove 'incompetent to establish a world-wide economic system', and can be only a stepping-stone to 'one world-wide socialist republic'.

A question on which Bukharin had formerly clashed with Lenin, whether the right of national self-determination was vested in the nation (even in the nation under bourgeois democracy)

as such, or whether it was limited to 'self-determination
for the workers', is cautiously handled. The party programme of
March 1919, while broadly accepting Lenin's thesis, had distinguished between nations belonging to two historical periods,
between nations 'evolving from mediaevalism to bourgeois
democracy' and nations evolving 'from bourgeois democracy to
Soviet or proletarian democracy'. *The ABC of Communism*
assumes that the major subject nationalities belong to the second
category, and therefore boldly proclaims that 'the right of the
nations to self-determination' means 'the right of the working
majority in any nation'. But it exhibits some embarrassment
about the rights of 'the backward and semi-savage peoples'. It
takes it for granted that, 'when socialism has been realized in the
more advanced countries of the world', these peoples will be only
too ready 'to join the general alliance of the peoples'. On the
other hand, the proletariat of the imperialist countries should
'leave to the natives of the backward lands the right to arrange
their own internal affairs as they please'; and the communist
party voices in these countries 'the demand for the national right
of self-determination'. In this question, as in others, *The ABC of
Communism* combines a utopian vision of the future – a world
society in which national differences are effaced – with concessions
to the expediencies of current policy.

A chapter of *The ABC of Communism* entitled 'The Second
and Third Internationals' opens with the bald statement: 'The
communist revolution can be victorious only as a world revolution.' This was the universal assumption of the Bolshevik leaders
at this time, and was in full accord with what Marx and Engels
had written. The prescriptions of the party programme of March
1919 did not go beyond the call 'to bring about the victory
of the world-wide proletarian revolution', 'to wage a pitiless
struggle against that bourgeois perversion of socialism which is
dominant in the leading official social-democratic and socialist
parties', and to recognize the newly formed Communist International as 'leader in the struggle of the proletariat for emancipation', spicing these injunctions with denunciations of supporters

of national defence, pacifists, jingo socialists, centrists, the League of Nations and the Second International, which was now 'merely a branch office of the League of Nations'. 'For the *proletariat*,' repeated Bukharin a few months later in the same international context, 'economic and political unity is a matter of life and death.'[1]

Since, however, the victory of world revolution in the early future was postulated, neither the party programme nor *The ABC of Communism* touched on international relations in the ordinary sense. The Brest-Litovsk crisis in the first months of 1918 had raised the problem of co-existence with an imperialist Power, and had been solved after a hard struggle, through the weight of Lenin's personal influence, in favour of the decision to accept the treaty. Bukharin had been at that time the foremost advocate of continuing to fight a 'revolutionary war'; and Preobrazhensky also belonged to the Left opposition. Now, more than a year later, when Germany had been wiped out, and the civil war against the 'Whites', supported by the western allies, was in full swing, the issues raised by Brest-Litovsk could be forgotten. 'The civil war is now conducted upon a world-wide scale [observed *The ABC of Communism*]. In part it takes the form of a war waged by bourgeois states against proletarian states.' More than another year elapsed before the introduction of NEP was logically matched by a compromise or a retreat (Lenin called NEP a 'retreat') in the conduct of international relations. The Anglo-Soviet trade treaty of March 1921, the Genoa conference, and the signature of the Rapallo Treaty with Germany in the spring of 1922, marked the beginning of a period of diplomatic activity in which peaceful co-existence with potentially hostile capitalist countries was accepted as the immediate goal of Soviet foreign policy.

*　　*　　*

The introduction of NEP in 1921 may, therefore, be said to have marked, among other things, the end of the Utopian period in

[1] Bukharin, *Ekonomika Perekhodnogo Perioda*, i 156.

Soviet history, in which Bukharin played a significant role, and of which *The ABC of Communism* is an outstanding memorial. It was a period during which the energies of politicians and administrators were absorbed by the civil war and by problems of survival, and the mass of the population exposed to intolerable hardships and to constant calls for superhuman effort. Such periods commonly inspire, side by side with the harsh realism of current experience, and by way of compensation for it, far-ranging visions of a future social order to be attained through the present turmoil of exertion and suffering, visions embodying the ideals for which the struggle is being waged. In such times of storm and stress the utopian elements inherent in any revolutionary doctrine are thrown into relief. If Lenin wrote *State and Revolution* in the interval between two revolutions, *The ABC of Communism* appeared at the most anxious moment of the civil war, when Soviet Russia was an isolated enclave in a hostile world, when the armies of Yudenich were massing for the attack on Petrograd and those of Denikin for the advance on Moscow. Little more than a year later the civil war had been won; and, after the momentary panic of the Kronstadt mutiny, the existence of the Soviet regime was no longer threatened. It found itself, almost suddenly, the uncontested heir to a vast devastated and disordered territory; and the single overwhelming task which confronted it was to restore order in the countryside and to bring food and fuel to the towns. Utopian visions of a future that now seemed inconceivably remote were irrelevant to this task. Bukharin symbolically abandoned the extreme of revolutionary idealism for the extreme of administrative prudence, completing in the next few years the transition from the far Left to the Right of the party, and making himself the principal theoretical apologist of 'Socialism in One Country'. A new era in the chequered history of the revolution had begun.

Such sharp distinctions can, however, be misleading. Many party stalwarts were uneasy at the shelving of revolutionary ideals and revolutionary aspirations under the crude impact of Stalinist realism. Down to the end of 1927 this uneasiness was kept alive by the semi-legal activities of opposition groups – not only the 'United Opposition' of Trotsky, Zinoviev and Kamenev, but survivors of the old 'Democratic Centralists' and 'Workers' Opposition'; and even the trade unions and the Komsomol sometimes spoke with discordant voices. After all opposition had been crushed, and party and state assumed monolithic forms, Stalin took over the drive for intensive industrialization once so vehemently preached by Trotsky. The campaign to industrialize and modernize the Soviet economy was conducted with the same impassioned appeals for ever-increasing effort, and the same contempt for hardships and sufferings incurred, which had been familiar in the civil war. Bukharin himself appealed to the congress of the Komsomol in 1928 in terms as eloquent and as utopian as can be found in any of his earlier writings:

> To give a meaning to all our construction, to make propaganda for full socialism and communism, propaganda for ways to attain it . . . must be the axis of our work. Only then can we create a certain emotion among the young, the emotion of construction; . . . only thus can we destroy that powerful prejudice which thinks that the heroic work of the proletariat is manifested only in fighting at the barricades or standing directly on the field of military action. This is untrue! The working class is heroic both when it fights and when it constructs the great human society of the future which the world does not yet know.[1]

Enormous pressures, and savage measures of compulsion, were employed to ensure the success of the campaign. But it could not have succeeded in the absence of a widespread undercurrent of idealism, a utopian vision of future triumphs to temper the nightmares of the present. No society entirely devoid of utopian aspirations will escape stagnation. Soviet society has not stagnated. In the long struggle over de-Stalinization in the 1950s and 60s, the old clash between passionate idealists and cautious administrators is again apparent. The theses on the seven-year plan presented by Khrushchev to the twenty-first party congress in 1958 revived

[1] *VIII Vsesoyuznyi S"ezd VLKSM* (1928) 31.

old utopian ingredients of the Marxist programme by announcing 'immediate new measures . . . to liquidate the essential differences between manual and intellectual labour, between town and country'. A report in the foreign Press in 1965 of an intention to re-publish *The ABC of Communism* in the USSR proved incorrect. But, if any such proposal was canvassed, it was symptomatic of a still living desire to recall earlier and more idealistic epochs of the party history. Long passages of the work are out of date and almost unreadable today: this is the common fate of Utopias of the past generation. But something of the spirit in which it was written is still alive. It remains to be seen whether it is strong enough to inspire action.

V *The Structure of Soviet Society*

A GOOD deal of attention has been given lately to the question of the structure of Soviet society. In a Third Programme broadcast[1] Professor Seton-Watson attempted to establish an analogy between the present ruling class in Soviet society and the ruling class of Victorian England. It was, he suggested, a 'state bourgeoisie' instead of a 'private bourgeoisie', but still a bourgeoisie – a bourgeois ruling class; and he went on to make comparisons between Soviet and Victorian tastes in architecture and music, to which he attributed a specifically bourgeois character. I may perhaps differ from Professor Seton-Watson less in substance than in terminology. But confused terminology leads to confused thinking: and I want to show here why I find his terminology misleading and to suggest some reflections of my own on the structure of Soviet society.

Let us agree, to start with, that every organized society, including Soviet society, throws up a ruling group. Let us also agree that contemporary Russia, like Victorian England, is the product of an industrial revolution. (Incidentally, Great Britain and Russia are the only two great countries which have carried out their industrial revolutions without the aid of foreign capital – a fact which may account for some of the unlovely features which have disfigured both.) I shall refrain from speculating about architecture or music. But it seems to me that it is this common background of industrial revolution which provides the explanation of certain analogies between Victorian literature and

[1] *The Listener*, 2 June 1955.

current Soviet literature. Both show the same crude moralizing tendencies, the same inclination to paint human conduct in sheer black and white, the same simple, unsophisticated eagerness to reward energy with success and to punish sloth with disgrace. Both inculcate the same virtues of industry and application in work and of respectability and restraint in living. These are the virtues which the ruling group in any rising industrial society will want to inculcate in the rank and file of its people – the duty to work as a service to the community, the duty to save, the duty not to squander resources. This is, broadly speaking, what the Victorians called leading 'a godly, righteous, and sober life'; and these are the ideals which Soviet moralists also infuse into Soviet literature for the edification of the Soviet worker.

These are no doubt what we commonly call bourgeois ideals or bourgeois values. But this merely begs the question. These are the ideals and slogans of the industrial revolution; some of them were inherited from an earlier phase of predominantly commercial capitalism. In Britain the industrial revolution, following hard on the French revolution, was associated economically with the rise of industrial capitalism and politically with the rise to power of the bourgeoisie or middle class. But in Russia the industrial revolution was associated with a totally different political revolution which inaugurated a totally different economic system. The revolution of 1917 overthrew not only what was left of the old landed aristocracy, but also the new rising industrial and commercial bourgeoisie; it put into power an entirely fresh group of rulers.

Quarrels about the use of words are generally pointless; and, if anyone wants to affix the bourgeois label to the ruling group of every industrial society and to define the word 'bourgeoisie' in that way, I suppose he is entitled to do so. But to call the Soviet ruling group a bourgeoisie seems to me to have two particular inconveniences. The first objection is that the words 'bourgeois' and 'bourgeoisie' have a specific, and in my view honourable, place in modern history. The bourgeoisie provided the driving power in that very great period of history which we sometimes call nineteenth-century civilization. Its twin pillars were the Rights of Man and the Wealth of Nations. It was the great age of the individual. All men were free and equal in the sense that all had equal civil rights. The sole function of the state was to guarantee and protect the enjoyment of those rights. Any collective conception of society was rejected. And the economic order was equally based on the free initiative of the individual in competition with other individuals: 'combination' was in principle something bad. In this economic order, private ownership occupied a central place; and this was partly because wealth was the reward and tangible evidence of virtue ('what is a man worth?' meant 'how much property does he have?'), and partly because ownership was the essential basis of that private enterprise which made the wheels of industry go round.

Property was for a long time the condition even of political rights: Marx described forms of property as 'the solid basis of the political organization'. And this was not a specifically Marxist view. To 'have a stake in the country', in the famous Victorian phrase, meant to own property. The last traces of the property-franchise did not disappear in this country till well on in the present century. Individual ownership was the basis of bourgeois civilization. 'Civil life', says Hauriou in the most famous French nineteenth-century text-book of jurisprudence, 'consists in the right to utilize (*faire valoir*) one's property'. It seems to me that a bourgeoisie which controls neither means of production nor commodities and draws profits neither from production nor from trade is a contradiction in terms. In Soviet Russia we are dealing with a system which, both in theory and practice, rejects every one of the characteristic values for which, historically, the bourgeoisie has stood.

The other objection which I see to this usage is that there was, and to some extent still is, an element in Soviet society which is by common consent properly called bourgeois. When Lenin described the social structure resulting from NEP, he referred to 'the co-operation of two classes – workers and peasants – to which are now admitted on certain conditions the nepmen, that is to say, the bourgeoisie'. For Lenin in 1921 the bourgeoisie consisted primarily of the nepmen: the next few years saw the rise of another bourgeois group in the country – the well-to-do peasants or kulaks. But the point is that these bourgeois elements in Soviet society – the nepmen and the kulaks – were outside the ruling group, and were in the position of members of society who enjoyed temporary toleration because the regime was not strong enough to do without them. It is true that in the middle 1920s some of the Bolshevik leaders, notably Bukharin and Rykov, for a time were indulgent to the claims of the kulaks. But this so-called Right opposition was put out of business in 1929. The introduction of the first five-year plan and the collectivization of the peasant sealed the issue. If Soviet Russia had been ruled by a bourgeoisie these events would have been inconceivable. The ruling group in Soviet society was decisively and irrevocably anti-bourgeois. There may even be bourgeois elements in Soviet society today – speculators, contact men, and private traders in town and country. But in so far as these bourgeois elements exist, it is notorious that they exist not because the ruling group likes them or wants them, but because it is not strong enough to get rid of them. There are enormous inequalities up and down the scale; the ruling group lives better, far better, than the masses. But this is characteristic of any ruling group in any kind of society. It does not entitle the ruling group in the Soviet Union to the bourgeois label.

But let us get away from these questions of terminology and look a little more closely at the composition of this ruling group. I will begin historically. The victors of 1917 thought they were establishing a dictatorship of the proletariat, or, a shade more realistically, a dictatorship of the proletariat and the peasantry. Just as the peasants were encouraged to seize the land, so the workers were encouraged to take over the factories. 'Workers' control' was the slogan of the hour. Workers' control did not work, and without it the dictatorship of the proletariat ceased to be a reality and became a symbol. It was replaced by what? The answer is clear. By the dictatorship of the party – the phrase was used at the time by Lenin and others, though afterwards rejected as heretical – and later by the dictatorship of the party machine. In other words, if we want to identify the ruling group in Soviet society, we have to look not for a class but for a party.

The Marxist class analysis of society was a product of the nineteenth century. Few people are convinced by the famous generalization with which the *Communist Manifesto* opens, that all history has been the history of class struggles. Marx took what he correctly diagnosed as the most significant feature of contemporary society in western Europe and sweepingly extended it to other periods, where its application was by no means so clear. Marx never explained what he meant by a class: it probably seemed so obvious a phenomenon of the world in which he lived as not to require definition. But its essence was plainly economic: class was determined by the relation of the persons concerned to the ownership of the means of production. Class is often used in English as the equivalent of social status. Marx did not understand it in this sense; and in Marx's sense there is no ruling class in the USSR today. There is a ruling group which finds its institutional embodiment in the party.

This is, I think, significant. A class is an economic formation, a party a political formation. I shall not argue that economic factors play a smaller role in the life of society today than in the nineteenth century. But what I would maintain is that the clear-cut line of demarcation between economics and politics which dominated all economic thinking in the nineteenth century, including that of Marx, is out of date. In Soviet Russia, at any rate, economics means politics, and the structure of Soviet society must be analysed in terms not of economic class but of political party.

As I have said, the dictatorship of the proletariat was replaced by the dictatorship of the party when workers' control collapsed in the factories. And workers' control collapsed because the workers lacked the necessary technical engineering and managerial skills. One of the first tasks of the party, of the ruling group, was to find the technicians and white-collar workers of all grades to put industry back into production; and the attitude to be adopted to these 'specialists', as they were called, was a constant preoccupation of party literature. And when, a few years later, the even more desperate problem was tackled of mechanizing agriculture and introducing modern methods of cultivation, the difficulty once more was to provide not only machinery, but skilled personnel to use it and to organize its use. It was precisely those specialists who, being indispensable to the regime, came to occupy a leading – and sometimes equivocal – position in the ruling group of what was still called a workers' state; and to study the attitude of the party to them is an important part of the analysis of Soviet society.

From the outset the attitude of the party to the specialists was quite different from its attitude to the nepmen. The nepman, and *a fortiori* the kulak, was *ex hypothesi* an enemy of the regime, pursuing aims incompatible with it, tolerated only so long as he had to be. A loyal nepman or a loyal kulak was an impossibility; no nepman or kulak could ever be admitted to the party. The specialist, on the other hand, though by his origins he might be a class enemy, like the nepman, was pursuing the aims of the regime whose servant he was. His origins might make him suspect. But he could be, and often was, loyal; and as time went on more and more specialists became party members. Thus, for the specialist, origin was not the determining factor. He might be bourgeois by origin but he was not bourgeois in function. He did not enjoy the economic independence of the entrepreneur. On the contrary, he was politically dependent on the government and on the party. If he was successful, success was rewarded not by increased profits, but by promotion to a bigger and better job. The soft-pedalling of world revolution, the proclamation of 'socialism in one country', and the policy of industrialization eased the process of the assimilation of the specialist. By the end of the 1920s he had become, by and large, a loyal servant of the regime; the avenues of promotion and of party membership were wide open to him.

I do not think that up to this time the specialist had any important influence on decisions of policy. These were still taken by the old party leadership, by the survivors of the pre-revolutionary

party intelligentsia. But in the 1930s, when a new generation grew up which had never known pre-revolutionary Russia,
and when sons of workers had clambered up the educational
ladder to the top, the distinctions began to fade. The taint of
bourgeois origin was no longer acutely felt; and the whole
group of white collar workers – party officials, government
officials, managers, technicians, teachers, doctors, lawyers, and
intellectuals of all kinds – began gradually to coalesce. Official
pronouncements began to extol the member of this new intelligentsia; the Stalin constitution enfranchised him irrespective of
his origin; the party statute of 1939 gave him a status in the party
side by side with the worker and the peasant.

It is in this new intelligentsia, recruited from different class
origins, and not constituting a class in the Marxist or Leninist
sense of the term, that we must look for the ruling group in
Soviet society. This is the group which has substituted itself for
the dictatorship of the proletariat; the only theoretical justification for the substitution is that its *raison d'être* and its purpose –
the cementing force which holds it together – is the industrialization of the country. In this respect, it still carries the dynamic of
the proletarian revolution; and to this long-term purpose the
immediate welfare of the worker, to say nothing of the peasant,
will be ruthlessly sacrificed. The ruling group remains pledged
to the eradication of everything bourgeois from Soviet society.
If it still tolerates a handful of nepmen, it tolerates them because
it must. It is engaged in a desperate uphill struggle to turn the
kolkhoz worker into a good socialist – a struggle only halted by
the still more desperate need to induce him to feed the towns for
a meagre return in the form of consumer goods. This is the core
of the problem which any ruling group that stands for industrialization has to face.

One more question: How far does this ruling group constitute a
closed and privileged social order? Professor Seton-Watson lays
stress on the growth of educational privilege. I think too much
can be made of this argument. Every ruling group looks after its
own, including its own children; and, when good educational

facilities are scarce, it will see to it that its children get the best. But the essential fact about Soviet society is that it is the society of an expanding economy; and educational facilities, too, are expanding rapidly. In an expanding society policies of exclusion do not work and do not last. The child of the worker does not, it is true, start level with the child of the party official or of the industrial manager. But the gulf is not unbridgeable, and it seems likely to narrow if the Soviet economy continues to expand at anything like its present rate. So long as this goes on, Soviet society and the ruling group will remain fluid and we shall see further changes. Meanwhile, we only confuse ourselves by attempting to equate the present regime in Russia with anything we have seen in the past – whether with a Tsarist autocracy or with a Victorian bourgeoisie. It is a new phenomenon in history, with new merits and new vices, and we had better try to see it for what it is.

VI Revolution from Above: The Road to Collectivization

THE decision taken at the end of 1929 to proceed to the mass collectivization of Soviet agriculture has always been something of a puzzle. Pronouncements of party leaders up to that time had given no reason to expect so far-reaching a measure. It was followed by disastrous consequences which had clearly not been foreseen, and which for some years altogether nullified its advantages. Granted that we now approach the problem with the benefit of hindsight, it remains a matter of legitimate speculation why this drastic solution was so precipitately adopted.

Many writers[1] have suggested that ideology may have been responsible for driving the Soviet leaders into action inappropriate to the situation which confronted them. Marx undoubtedly believed in the efficiency of large-scale collective organization for agriculture as for industry; and he held that the peasant would eventually be obliged to abandon his reactionary role as a petty proprietor and enter the ranks of the proletariat. But he evidently regarded this not as something to be enforced on the peasant, but as a natural corollary of the revolutionary process. Engels, after Marx's death, in his pamphlet on *The Peasant Question in France and Germany*, explicitly ruled out the idea of 'expropriating the small peasants [as opposed to the large landowners] by force, with or without compensation':

> Our task in relation to the small peasants will consist, first and foremost, in converting their private production and private

[1] D. Mitrany, *Marx against the Peasant* (1961) *passim*; A. Nove in *Soviet Studies*, April 1959, p. 386.

ownership into collective production and ownership – not, however, by forcible means but by example and by offering social aid for this purpose.

This very specific passage was more than once quoted by Lenin both before and after the revolution, and was familiar to every Bolshevik. Even at the eighth party congress, held at the height of the civil war in March 1919, where Lenin remarked that 'we have been, are, and shall be in a state of direct civil war with the kulaks', he deplored the fact that blows intended for kulaks had sometimes fallen on middle peasants; and the resolution of the congress, drafted by Lenin, firmly enunciated the principle of non-violence in regard to the middle peasant:

> In encouraging associations of every kind, and also agricultural communes, of middle peasants, the representatives of the Soviet power should not permit the slightest compulsion in founding such bodies. . . . Those representatives of the Soviet power who allow themselves to apply not merely direct, but even indirect, compulsion in order to attach peasants to communes, should be held strictly accountable and removed from work in the countryside.

Throughout the middle 1920s, collectivization remained in the party programme, but as a distant and unrealizable goal; even Molotov is on record as referring in 1925[1] to 'poor peasant illusions about the collectivization of the broad peasant masses'. The opposition platform of September 1927 put forward, without special emphasis and without any hint of the use of force, its routine demand for a gradual advance towards a socialized agriculture.

With the turn to the Left at the end of 1927, more talk was heard of collectivization, and the fifteenth party congress in December 1927 proclaimed 'an offensive against the kulak'. But this did not imply any intention to use force. When a foreign delegate asked Stalin in November 1927 how he hoped 'to realize collectivism in the peasant question', he spoke of 'measures of an

[1] *Pravda*, 9 May 1925.

economic, financial and cultural-political character', and concluded: 'things are moving in that direction, but have not yet
got, and will not soon get, so far'. At the congress Stalin attacked
'those comrades [presumably members of the opposition] who
think it possible and necessary to to finish with the kulaks by
administrative measures, through the GPU'; and Molotov, ex-
plaining that the party was still faithful to NEP, went on: 'The
affair can proceed only by way of the gradual development of
large collective farms. . . . We can permit of no illusions, no
coercion in regard to the peasantry in the transition to large-scale
farming.'

Even after the severe grain crisis of the first months of 1928,
no thought of mass collectivization by force entered the mind
even of the most ambitious planners. The framers of the first
five-year plan, drafted in the autumn of 1928, made what
were thought to be optimistic prognostications of the advance of
the 'socialized sector of agriculture', but frankly admitted that
'we should deceive ourselves if we claimed that the socialized
sector, in the dimensions in which it will exist at the end of the
five-year period, will enable us to neglect the production which
will be brought to the market by groups of middle peasants'.
Pravda on 2 November 1928 denounced 'ignorant attempts to
solve the complex question of the conquest of capitalist elements
in the countryside by administrative measures', and as late as
2 June 1929 demanded in a banner headline 'Neither terror nor
dekulakization, but a socialist offensive along the paths of NEP'.
At the sixteenth party conference in April 1929 a sharp controversy occurred on the question whether to admit kulaks to the
kolkhozy. If admitted, they might dominate and pervert the
kolkhoz; if excluded, they would remain as independent producers in competition with the kolkhozy. No alternative was
envisaged. A commentator in *Bol'shevik* remarked ironically:
'We have heard no proposals to drive the kulak off the land, or to
send him packing to desert frontier regions or to an uninhabited
island.' The aim of Soviet policy, Kalinin told the fifth union
congress of Soviets in May 1929, was not only to promote

collective agriculture, but to improve 'the individual poor and middle peasant economy'.[1]

Whatever prompted the decision abruptly taken in December 1929, nobody seriously contemplated it six months earlier or thought of it as required by party doctrine. It was only in December 1929 that Stalin tried to explain away the famous passage from Engels on the ground that it was written under a regime of private property in land; he did not mention Lenin's, or his own earlier, pronouncements on the subject. Marxist dogma favoured collectivization in principle. But it would be absurd to suggest that it was dogma which drove the politicians to act as they did.

Industrialization did not become an issue till 1925, when pre-war levels had been regained and most existing factories and machines brought back into production. The question of the rate of further expansion now became acute. 1926 was the year of the inception of Dnieprostroi, and 1927 of the Stalingrad tractor factory. Preobrazhensky had demonstrated in his famous article on 'primitive socialist accumulation' at the end of 1924 that expansion could be financed only by extracting 'surpluses' from the peasant; and, though this did not become official doctrine till 1928 (when Stalin spoke of exacting 'tribute' from the peasantry), it was not seriously refuted. But in 1925–26 it was assumed that industrialization would proceed at a pace which would not place too great a strain on the peasant, and that emphasis would fall on the production of consumer goods for the peasant market. Dzerzhinsky, who was president of Vesenkha till his death in July 1926, strongly upheld these principles, and Pyatakov, who wanted more intensive industrialization, was dismissed. An important factor was the international crisis and the war scare of the spring and summer of 1927 (disaster in China, breaking-off of relations by Great Britain), which focused attention on the need for rapid industrialization and for emphasis on the heavy capital goods industries which were the basis of military strength.

[1] 5 *S"ezd Sovetov SSSR* (1929) no. 15, p. 3.

From 1927 onwards industrialization was the overriding official aim. It was affirmed by the fifteenth party congress in December 1927, and led to the rift with the Right wing in the party (Bukharin) in 1928–29. The views of the Right, as Mr Barrington Moore has remarked, 'strongly resembled the gradualist views of western social-democracy';[1] and this doubtless explains the favour commonly shown to Bukharin by western writers. At a moment when the survival of the revolution seemed to be in jeopardy both from 'capitalist' intervention from without and from the growing strength of 'capitalist' elements in the economy, such a policy was unlikely to find acceptance. It was recalled that Bukharin had once in an incautious moment spoken of 'snail's pace industrialization'. This was now out of date. Nothing would suffice but intensive industrialization at all costs – even the cost of maximum pressure on the peasant (and on the industrial worker). Meanwhile every problem was aggravated by the growing imbalance between industry and agriculture. The value of the output of industry increased by 34·2 per cent in 1926, by 13·3 per cent in 1927, and 19 per cent in 1928; the corresponding figures for the output of agriculture were 7·5, 2·5 and 2·5 per cent (it actually fell by 2·4 per cent in 1929).[2] The facts were worse than these figures indicated; for the proportion of wheat and rye, the principal food crops, in the total output, and the proportion of these crops brought to the market, were both declining. While industry raced ahead, agriculture was not advancing fast enough even to take account of the needs of a rising population.

While, however, much can be said for treating collectivization as a by-product or necessary condition of industrialization, this is not the whole story. NEP was a compromise between nationalized industry and individual peasant farming, between state control and a market economy, based on the survival of private capital. It represented a balance of forces in which the revolution had carried the towns and factories and the urban proletariat,

[1] Barrington Moore, *Soviet Politics* (1950) 103.
[2] *Narodnoe khozyaistvo SSSR v 1958 godu* (1959) 135, 351.

and had failed to carry the peasant countryside. Nobody expected the compromise to last for ever; the scissors crisis of 1923 and the persistent battle between controlled and 'free' prices were symptoms of the intensity of the underlying struggle. Either the nationalized industry through the medium of planning would succeed in subordinating the peasant economy to itself and integrating it into a centrally planned and centrally controlled system; or peasant resistance would prove impregnable and would compel state industry to operate within the framework of a market economy, in which even existing forms of control (e.g. the monopoly of foreign trade) might be progressively modified or dismantled.

If we free ourselves from the hindsight conferred by knowledge of the sequel, we can see that in the middle 1920s the issue was still open. In 1924 Zinoviev coined the slogan 'Face to the Countryside'; and, when in 1925 Bukharin issued the injunction 'Enrich yourselves' to 'all the peasants', the phrase was disowned, but not the policy. Removal of controls (e.g. on the leasing of land and the hiring of labour) favoured the well-to-do and efficient peasant, exactly as the Stolypin reform had done; its logic was the creation of small rural capitalists. This policy was repeatedly challenged by the opposition, which Zinoviev had now joined; the so-called 'declaration of the 83' of May 1927 alleged that the 'real danger' to the regime now came from the kulak 'under the brand-name of the economically strong peasant'. As Trotsky put it, 'the wager on the *capitalist farmer* (the European or American-ized kulak)' might well yield fruits, but they would be 'capitalist fruits which at no distant stage will lead to the political downfall of the Soviet power'.[1] This was the policy which was supported by the 'expert' advisers of Narkomfin and Narkomzem, most of them pre-revolutionary professors or officials. These fell into two groups. The liberal-bourgeois group (Kondratiev, Litoshenko) sought to encourage investment in agriculture, as the sector of the economy likely to yield most rapid returns, rather than in heavy industry, to remove restrictions designed to favour or

[1] *Byulleten' Oppozitsii* (Paris) no. 1–2, July 1929, p. 22.

protect the poor peasant, and to restore as much as possible of a free market economy; this would promote maximum production by the most efficient peasants. The neo-narodnik group (Chayanov, Chelintsev, Makarov) was against the kulak or the small rural capitalist, and in principle supported equalization of holdings, but believed that the small peasant farm was the only sound basis for agriculture, and resisted any policy designed to create large-scale units of cultivation. Both groups were united in their opposition to measures of state control and to collective forms of agriculture promoted by official action. These groups were put out of action early in 1928. Bukharin, when he took up the campaign against pressure on the peasant, followed a recognizably similar course, and, though he never made a clear choice between 'liberal' and 'neo-narodnik' lines of approach, and was stronger on the negative than on the positive side, was discredited by his association with these heretical doctrines. In this welter of opinion the need for some kind of action was apparent; and any action involved coming down on one side of the fence or the other.

The crisis occurred in the winter of 1927–28, simultaneously with acceptance of the policy of rapid industrialization, and for reasons in part independent of it. The harvests of 1925 and 1926 were good. The official grain collections proceeded satisfactorily, and the needs of government, cities, and factories were met. Numerous private traders still operated in grain, but in relatively small amounts, and at prices not much higher than the official prices. It was assumed that better organization would make the official collections still more efficient and that the private trader would be gradually squeezed out. Some food shortages in the cities in the early summer of 1927 were attributed to increased consumption or to hoarding rather than to difficulties of supply. But another good harvest in 1927 (only slightly below the bumper harvest of 1926) underlined the deep-seated character of the difficulties. In the autumn shortages became chronic; the grain collections fell off catastrophically; and the opposition, now in the last stages of open activity, made capital out of the failure of the policy of support for the well-to-do peasant, alias the kulak.

The two main elements in the problem were soon apparent, and were somewhat guardedly discussed at the fifteenth party congress in December 1927 (which expelled the opposition from the party).

In the first place the productivity of Soviet agriculture was too low; tables were circulated at this time showing how far it lagged behind that of the rest of Europe and of the Americas. It was difficult to think of raising productivity by mechanization or by scientific methods of farming unless the existing 'fragmentation' of the land – its division among 25 million small peasant *dvors* – could be overcome. This could theoretically be achieved in two ways – by encouraging the 'strong' peasant to acquire more land and more control of the tools of production (the 'capitalist' solution), or by collective organization of agriculture (the 'socialist' solution). Secondly, the marketability (tovarnost') of the crop was too low. Of the 1926 harvest only 16·9 per cent was marketed, i.e. became available to feed the urban population, against a pre-war figure of 24 per cent. This was also the result of having too many too small holdings; it was the peasant who held most land and most machines who, like the former landowner, brought most grain to the market. But in the grain collections of 1927–28 a new and disturbing factor appeared. After the third good harvest in succession, the most efficient and well-to-do peasants, having complied with Bukharin's injunction 'Enrich ourselves', were more prosperous than at any time since the revolution. They had not only stocks of grain, but money; and, owing to the emphasis on production of capital goods, the consumer goods on which the money might have been spent were in chronically short supply. With memories of past inflation they preferred to use money to pay their taxes and t hoard their grain; official grain prices were low, and they reasonably calculated that they would gain by waiting. The grain collections for November and December 1927 were only half those of the previous year.

Once the party congress was over, the gravity of the situation was realized, and the party leaders were seized with panic. Early in January 1928 an instruction was sent to party organizations

everywhere to bring in the grain at any cost. The leaders themselves toured key regions; Stalin went to Siberia – the only such
mission undertaken by him after Lenin's death. What were
called 'extraordinary measures' were applied. These included
forced loans, 'self-taxation', prosecutions under an article of the
code imposing penalties for concealment of grain, allocation of
quotas, and more or less open requisition, though any analogy
with the methods of war communism was vigorously denied by
the authorities, and some of the things done were afterwards
described as abuses. It was proof of the large stocks of grain in
peasant hands at this time that these methods were for the
moment entirely successful. The grain collections of January–
March 1928 were far in excess of any corresponding period, and
wiped out the large deficits of the previous six months. When the
agricultural year ended on 30 June 1928, the grain collections
fell only a little below the total of 1926–27, and the collections
of wheat and rye (the main food crops) equalled it. But the costs
were heavy. The peasants had been stripped of their reserves, so
that the operation could never be repeated; few managed to keep
more than was barely necessary to carry them through to the
next harvest; some went hungry, or had to kill their animals.
The operation was a declaration of war against the kulak,[1] who
would henceforth fight the authorities by any means in his
power. Moreover the blows had fallen on many who could not
by any stretch of imagination be called kulaks – on middle
peasants, on anyone who had some reserve of grain. On the other
side, the authorities drew the short-sighted conclusion that
strong-arm methods paid. This episode, more than any other
single event, set in motion the process which ended in collectivization. It was a decisive turning-point.

In 1928–29 a marked decline for the first time occurred in the
sowings of wheat and rye, presumably owing to the reluctance

---

[1] No satisfactory definition of a kulak could be found, and the word was
applied as a term of propaganda to any peasant holding, or believed to hold,
grain surplus to his immediate requirements. Estimates of the total number of
kulaks, and of the proportion of grain delivered by kulaks and middle peasants,
vary widely and become almost meaningless.

of the well-to-do peasant to grow surpluses which were liable to confiscation. The prospects of the grain collections were grim. Violent arguments were exchanged at the party central committee; and against the view of Stalin (who seems to have been converted to a tough line by his Siberian trip) it was decided in July 1928 to raise official grain prices by 10–15 per cent. The harvest was patchy – poor in the Ukraine and the northern Caucasus (important rye and wheat areas), good elsewhere. In the end the total yield was not far below that of 1928. The rise in official prices helped the collections at first. But private market prices again quickly overtook them. In the grain collections of 1928–29 the private trader paid two or three times the official prices for wheat and rye. By 1 April 1929, private retail prices of foodstuffs were already double the prices in state or co-operative shops, and continued to soar. 'We are entering a period', said Kalinin in May 1929, 'in which capitalist elements oppose the most furious resistance to the advance of socialism.'[1] By this time no peasant who had access to the private market would deliver grain to the official collectors except under compulsion; and the old 'extraordinary measures' were again in use. But this time the results were trivial. The total of the grain collections for 1928–29 (in round figures) was 8 million tons against 10 millions for 1927–28, of wheat and rye 5 millions against 8 millions. This was near starvation level for the cities; nobody could survive any longer without paying the exorbitant prices of the private market. It became necessary to import 250,000 tons of grain. It should be emphasized that in the summer of 1929 the system of official grain collections had effectively broken down, though nobody would publicly admit it, and that, under existing conditions, no reasonable prospect existed of restoring it. A third successive annual crisis of the grain collections loomed ahead. The problem of supplying towns and factories had become completely intractable. Gradualism was not enough. This was the negative impulse behind the decision to collectivize.

Lenin's dictum about the 100,000 tractors which could convert

[1] 5 *S"ezd Sovetov SSSR* (1929) no. 15, p. 37.

the peasant to communism was the winged word which inspired
the programme of mechanization plus collectivization. The im-
portation of American tractors went on throughout the 1920s.
The building of the Stalingrad tractor factory began in 1928.
The year 1927 saw the foundation of the first large-scale grain-
growing Sovkhozy and kolkhozy, mainly in the southern Ukraine
and the northern Caucasus. The Shevchenko Sovkoz in the
Odessa province was the first 'grain-factory' with its attached
fleet of tractors; and here the first Machine Tractor Station
(MTS) was created in 1928 to serve not only the Sovkhoz itself
but neighbouring peasant holdings. The programme was based
on the correct calculation that higher yields could be obtained
by these methods than from individual peasant holdings, and
above all that the 'marketability' of the crop, the proportion
available for the towns and factories, would be substantially
increased. This was a sensible policy. Belief in its potentialities
was the positive impulse behind the materially premature decision to collectivize. The failure of the grain collections convinced
the leaders that collectivization was necessary. Mechanization
convinced them it was possible. The desperation bred by the
first conviction may have contributed to the optimism of the
second.

The weakness of the policy was that, though a real beginning
had been made, mechanization had scarcely progressed far enough
to sustain the weight of widespread collectivization. The first
tractors did not come off the production line in Stalingrad till
1930; another tractor factory was planned in Chelyabinsk, but
was still in the future. A dozen or more large-scale Sovkhozy and
kolkhozy were at work. But, even so, the total number of those
incorporated in all Sovkhozy and kolkhozy together amounted in
1929 only to 5·4 per cent of the peasant population; they were
responsible for 14 per cent of marketable production. This included many small Sovkhozy and kolkhozy whose productivity
was little or no higher than that of peasant holdings. By and large,
the country was still overwhelmingly dependent on primitive
individual peasant agriculture. Peasants whose holdings were

incorporated in the Shevchenko Sovkhoz retained vegetable and garden plots for their own use. Kalinin explained that this was because they had 'a great deal of free time thanks to the complete mechanization' of farm work.[1] Moreover, all these institutions – notably the tractor and the MTS – were still in the stage of teething troubles. As a later commentator put it, 'the road from the wooden plough to the tractor' had been 'only half travelled' even at the end of the first five-year plan.[2] But, where there is only one way out of a desperate situation, it must be tried even with inadequate resources. This was the mood of the decision of December 1929.

The short history of the Communist Party published in 1938 and credited to Stalin described collectivization as a revolution carried out 'from above, on the initiative of the State power, with direct support from below'. (I have found no earlier use of the phrase in this context.) This has now been condemned as heretical on the ground that it relegates to a secondary place 'the decisive force in the revolutionary transformation of the countryside – the movement of the toiling masses themselves'.[3] Contemporary evidence is scarce. The existence of class divisions in the country-side, and the hostility of the poor peasant to the kulak, were postulates of party doctrine and policy from Lenin onwards: it was one of Bukharin's sins that he failed to recognize these divisions, and treated the peasantry as an undifferentiated mass. What was referred to as the policy of 'kindling the class war in the countryside' was actively pursued, for the first time since the civil war, in the grain collections crisis of January–March 1928. It was promised that 25 per cent of all grain confiscated under the article of the code prohibiting concealment of grain would be handed over to the poor peasants in the form of long-term credits. This was designed to encourage informers, and doubtless did so; without local informers the large stocks collected during these

[1] 5 *S"ezd Sovetov SSSR* (1929) no. 19, p. 3.
[2] *Istoriya Sovetskogo Krest'yanstva i Kolkhoznogo Stroitel'stva v SSSR* (1963) 201–2.
[3] *Voprosy Istorii KPSS*, 1964, no. 11, pp. 134–5; Stalin is blamed, ibid. p. 137, for 'an unjustified forcing of collectivization'.

months could hardly have been unearthed.

The expected result of deepening the rift between the kulak and the mass of the peasantry does not, however, seem to have followed to any significant extent. When hunger spread over the countryside, it was still the well-to-do peasant who had whatever grain was left, and who was therefore in a dominant position *vis-à-vis* the rest of the peasantry. Frumkin, in his letter to the party Central Committee of June 1928, wrote that the peasantry with few exceptions had turned against the party. This was denounced as heresy. But Bauman, secretary of the Moscow party committee and a staunch left-winger, also wrote in *Bol'shevik*[1] that 'the poor peasant, having nothing to eat, has had to do obeisance to the kulak', and that recent changes in the village had been 'not to our advantage, but to that of the kulaks'. More serious was the alienation of the middle peasants on whom much of the weight of the extraordinary measures had fallen. This was the gist of Bukharin's argument at the party central committee in July 1928. The kulak himself was not dangerous: 'We can shoot him down with machine-guns, and he cannot shake our country.' The danger was that the middle peasant would follow the kulak. The coining of the word *podkulachniki* (little sub-kulaks) for hangers-on of the kulaks from other strata of the peasantry points to the frequency of the phenomenon. There is little doubt that the party, in drawing a largely imaginary line between the kulak and the middle peasant, underestimated the degree of solidarity among different strata of the peasantry. Far from being gratified by the penalization of their old enemies the kulaks, the middle and even the poor peasants had reason to fear that the same penalties would fall on them. The archives report the 'spontaneous dekulakization' of 40 per cent of kulak holdings in the Lower Volga region in the winter of 1929–30.[2] But this, whatever exactly it may mean, seems to have been a rare exception. The official thesis, voiced by Kalinin, that encouragement by the government of collective and co-operative activities had

---

[1] *Bol'shevik*, 31 July 1928, no. 13–14, pp. 46–7.
[2] *Istoriya SSSR*, 1958, no. 6, p. 18.

'implanted in the peasantry a consciousness of collectivization', and an awareness of its benefits, had little foundation.[1] In general, the party and the government proceeded to the work of collectivization with a minimum of assistance from any group of the peasantry. The human, as well as the mechanical, resources available were inadequate to the smooth performance of the task.

When the party Central Committee at its session of November 1929 declared that 'the kolkhoz movement now presents to particular regions the task of wholesale collectivization', an early advance in certain localities was evidently envisaged. A recent article based on unpublished archives[2] gave some account of the background of the decision of December 1929. On 5 December a commission was set up by the party Central Committee to submit to the Politburo a plan of collectivization. The commission worked in eight sub-commissions, and on 22 December presented its report to the Politburo. This proposed collectivization by stages to be completed (except for Central Asia, Transcaucasia, and some northern regions) within the period of the first five-year plan. The Crimea and the Lower Volga region were to be collectivized in 1930; the North Caucasian, Middle Volga, and the Black Earth regions, and the steppe region of the Ukraine in 1931; Siberia, Kazakhstan, the Moscow and Nizhny-Novgorod regions, and the Ukraine on the left bank of the Dnieper in 1932. The collectives were to take the form of artels; land, machines, and working animals were to be included, but the peasant was to retain small animals and milch-cows serving his own use. When the report came before the Politburo Stalin demanded a speeding-up of the time-table, and the inclusion of all animals. On 3 January 1930, the commission submitted to the Politburo a revised plan on these lines. On this occasion Ryskulov, apparently with Stalin's support, called for a further speeding up and collectivization 'without any

[1] 5 *S"ezd Sovetov SSSR* (1929) no. 15, p. 28.
[2] *Voprosy Istorii KPSS*, 1964, no. 1, pp. 32–43; the only other reference which I have found to these proceedings is ibid., 1958, no. 4, p. 80, where one of the sub-commissions is said to have reported unanimously that 'the time is ripe to raise in more concrete form the question of the liquidation of the kulaks'.

limitations'. A decision was taken in this sense, and formed the basis of the published decision of the Central Committee of 5 January 1930, in which only a trace of the old staging remained in the provision that the Lower and Middle Volga regions, and the North Caucasus, would be collectivized by the autumn of 1930 or the spring of 1931, and the rest a year later. This account is no doubt correct as far as it goes. But nothing is quoted textually and the selective use of unpublished archives can be misleading. What we have here is perhaps something less than the whole truth. It does, however, reveal the haphazard and impulsive character of the final decision.

VII *Reflections on Soviet Industrialization*

NOBODY will doubt that industrialization is a major problem of the contemporary world, or that Soviet power and prestige owe much to the process of industrialization carried out in the USSR. The purpose of the present paper is not to examine the achievements, the failures or the costs of Soviet industrialization, but rather to investigate its specific place in the framework or perspective of industrialization considered as a historical phenomenon making its appearance in different contexts of time and space.

Much attention has recently been given by western writers – not without a side glance at current problems of industrialization in Asia and Africa – to Russian industrialization as an instance of industrialization in a 'backward' economy. Any country embarking on industrialization is in one sense, by definition, 'backward'. But something more than this is clearly meant. Gerschenkron, who has elaborated this theme at length in his collection of essays *Economic Backwardness in Historical Perspective*, distinguishes between the British, German and Russian types of industrialization, the British type being treated as the norm in relation to which the German, and *a fortiori* the Russian, types are economically backward. (American industrialization, which Gerschenkron does not discuss, presumably conforms to the British type.) Germany, and *a fortiori* Russia, on the threshold of industrialization were countries 'where the basic elements of backwardness appear in such an accentuated form as to lead to the use of essentially different institutional instruments of industrialization' (p. 16). The key to the institutional differences Gerschenkron finds in the fact that, while British industrialization was the product of individual entrepreneurial decisions, the German type (of which French industrialization was a variant) placed the main initiative in the hands of the banks. 'The continental practices in the field of industrial investment banking must be conceived as specific instruments of industrialization in a backward country.' (p. 14.) The Russian type represented a further stage of backwardness. The state substituted itself for the banks as 'the *agens movens* of industrialization'; indeed, 'the policies pursued by the Russian government in the nineties resembled closely those of the banks in Central Europe'. This was partly the result of military policies, especially of strategic railway construction. But 'these policies only reinforced and accentuated the basic tendencies of industrialization in conditions of economic backwardness' (p. 20). When we reach the Soviet period things are still worse. 'The Soviet experiment in rapid industrialization' followed 'a pattern of economic development which before the First World War seemed to have been relegated to the role of a historical museum piece'; it was something 'anachronistic, or rather parachronistic' – which did not, however, prevent it from proving 'immensely effective' (p. 149).

The distinctions thus drawn between British, German and Russian experience are for the most part valid and suggestive. But in a work which professes to place economic backwardness 'in historical perspective', a more critical look at the perspective may be appropriate. Some romantic nostalgia for the earlier (British) type of industrialization may be condoned. What is less admirable is the attempt to treat it as a model which later industrializations failed to follow. Though Gerschenkron disclaims any intention of setting up a norm of industrialization, the application of a criterion of backwardness inevitably leads to this result. 'The industrial history of Europe appears not as a series of mere repetitions of the "first" industrialization, but as an orderly system of graduated deviations from that industrialization.' (p. 44.) One of his favourite concepts is 'substitution' with its implication of the inferior

or factitious; in Russian industrialization 'these government's
budgetary policy was effectively *substituted* for the deficient internal market' (p. 126). The Russian type was a deviation
from the German type which was itself a deviation from the
British.

Great Britain provided the first recognized modern example of
the historical phenomenon which we know as industrialization;
and nineteenth-century writers, including Marx, treated British
industrialization as a sort of *Ur*-Industrialization from which the
process spread to other leading countries. But this went with an
acute consciousness of the darker sides of what came to be known
as the 'Industrial Revolution'.[1] The orthodox nineteenth-century
view (Toynbee, the Hammonds, the Webbs) was that its immediate effect was to impose severe sufferings and hardships on
the worker. This did not preclude the view that its ultimate effect
on the worker was beneficial (though this was denied by the
Marxists): the orthodox pre-1914 economic historian Cunningham wrote of 'the inevitable difficulties of transition' and of 'the
terrible suffering which was endured in the period of transition'.[2]
It would have seemed at this time paradoxical to hold up the
British process of industrialization as a model or norm from
which other industrializing countries would diverge to their
detriment. On the contrary, other countries were congratulated
on having been lucky enough, as late-comers, to avoid some of the
worst evils of the British industrial revolution.

The consequences of industrialization for the British working
class have recently been the subject of sharp controversy and
rapidly changing attitudes, ably summarized by R. M. Hartwell
a few years ago in an article in the *Journal of Economic History*.[3]
The argument took a characteristic and instructive course. In the
1920s a number of economists and economic historians (Clapham,
Hutt, Gregory) minimized or denied even the short-term suffer-

---

[1] For the origin of the term see G. N. Clark, *The Idea of the Industrial
Revolution* (Glasgow 1953).

[2] W. Cunningham, *The Growth of English Industry and Commerce* (Cambridge
1925) ii 668, 617, quoted by R. M. Hartwell (see below).

[3] Vol. xix (1959) no. 2, pp. 229–49.

ings inflicted on the workers by the introduction of the English factory system (the term 'revolution' was now avoided). In the 1930s the controversy was 'relatively quiescent'. In 1948 Professor Ashton returned to the defence of capitalism against the charge of having inflicted intolerable hardships on the industrial worker, and has since been followed by an ever growing host of disciples and imitators. (Among American intellectuals a similar rehabilitation of big business has been undertaken, having been inaugurated by articles in *Fortune* of December 1949 and April 1952.) Hartwell sagely concludes: 'Interpretations of the industrial revolution in England have not depended entirely on unbiased analysis of the evidence; to an important extent they have resulted from particular attitudes towards social, political and economic change.'

One could have been explicit. Before 1914 English industrial society was self-assured enough to digest without discomfort any criticism of its origins. The traumatic experience of the Russian revolution of 1917 put it on the defensive, made it sensitive to such criticism, and rendered the conception of revolution distasteful. It became invidious to agree with Marx, or to write the same things about English economic history as were written by Soviet historians. This was the mood of the 1920s. In the 1930s, by way of reaction against Hitler, the climate of opinion became temporarily more sympathetic to Marxism and to the Soviet Union; and a truce was called in the battle of the English industrial revolution. After the Second World War, opinion again turned sharply against the Soviet Union and against Marxism; and the view that the English industrial revolution had inflicted hardship and suffering on the worker was once more unacceptable. The chronology makes it clear that these writers were not primarily concerned with British industrialism. No doubt unconsciously – for historians rarely know what they are up to – they mirrored successive changes in attitude to Soviet industrialization. In order to show this up as a falling away from the original British model, any attempt to equate the two processes must be warded off; the threatened *tu quoque* must be refuted. It is interesting to note in passing that, while the American argument convicts Soviet industrialization of 'backwardness' on the ground of its failure to maintain private enterprise, the British argument does the same on the ground of its failure to live up to the humanitarian standards of British industrialization.

These controversies are none of my present business. I shall not attempt to contest the advantages of private enterprise or the view that Soviet industrialization was responsible for the deaths of more people, or made more people more unhappy, or raised standards of living more slowly, than British industrialization. Such arguments, taken by themselves, do not seem to me to lead anywhere. Nostalgia for the past seldom makes for good history. Any perspective based on the explicit or unspoken assumption that the initial British industrialization through private enterprise and the market was a 'normal' or 'advanced' mode of industrialization, from which 'backward' countries have regrettably, though perhaps to some extent unavoidably, diverged, seems to me not only highly idiosyncratic but essentially unhistorical. It might indeed be claimed that the concept 'normal' has here no meaning, and that, viewed historically, twentieth-century Soviet industrialization is more 'advanced' than any eighteenth- or nineteenth-century industrialization, not in any moral or political sense, and not merely in a temporal sense, but in the sense in which automated production in a large factory is more 'advanced' than production with hand tools in a small workshop.

The crucial point about the beginning of the process of industrialization is the character and origin of the resources needed to set it in motion. Great Britain and the Soviet Union are alike (and unlike most other industrial countries) in having industrialized without the benefit of foreign capital. In both countries, the industrial revolution was facilitated by an agricultural revolution and by the establishment of a primitive mining industry, and would scarcely have been possible without these assets. In most other respects Soviet industrialization diverged so far from British industrialization that it serves little purpose to regard the latter as a model. These divergences were due mainly to the difference in time, but partly also to the legacy of earlier Russian experiments in industrialization.

The first experiment was the work of Peter the Great. This, though it had its precedents in seventeenth-century western Europe, was so remote from the classical pattern of 'industrialization' afterwards set by the English eighteenth-century industrial revolution that it is commonly ignored in discussions of the subject. Peter the Great's industries worked exclusively on government orders (though some of the establishments were in private ownership), and fell into three groups: iron works producing armaments and military equipment; textile factories producing uniforms for the army and sail cloth for the navy; and a building industry engaged on public works of various kinds. Conscious imitation of western Europe, and desire to emulate western power, were major factors in these foundations. The labour employed was peasant serf labour drafted in large numbers into these new industrial occupations. Technical processes were primitive and undeveloped; capital equipment was at the outset negligible. Some of the industry created by Peter declined or collapsed after his death.[1] But some of it survived and set the pattern of Russian industrial development for a century and a half. Historical traditions and habits of mind die hard; and it is in survivals of a primitive Petrine conception of industrialization (and of the primitive economic conditions which went with it) rather than in the modern clash between 'market' and 'planning' conceptions of industrialization that we should look for traces of Russian 'backwardness'.

The second phase of Russian industrialization began in the second half of the nineteenth century, and was marked by three major developments. The emancipation of the serfs opened the way to the creation of a 'free' labour market and of an industry employing 'workers' in a modern sense. The arrival of the railway age in Russia had paved the way for large schemes of railway

[1] A. Kahan in *Journal of Economic History*, xxv (Mar 1965) no. 1, pp. 61–85, argues that the decline has been exaggerated by Russian historians anxious to minimize Peter's achievement.

construction, dictated mainly by military needs, but relying on foreign materials and foreign example. The growth of a large potential consumer market led to the establishment of a mass textile industry using foreign machinery and foreign technicians. These three developments were overtaken by, and merged in, the wave of intensive industrialization through foreign investment (including foreign loans to the Russian government) which swept over Russia in the fifteen years following the conclusion of the Franco-Russian alliance in 1891. Since the aim was to build up Russian military strength, investment through state channels was directed primarily to the heavy and capital goods industries (including communications), and state orders rather than the market dictated the character of the end product. In brief, this phase of Russian industrialization had the following characteristics:

(1) It was set in motion and directed by the state. Much of it (including railway construction) satisfied military needs; many of the foreign loans which financed it were governmental loans granted for political motives.

(2) Its normal form was the large unit working with complex modern machines and requiring large capital investment.

(3) It was concerned primarily with industries producing capital goods, not consumer goods. This was only partly due to military needs and to those of railway construction; in a period of advanced technology, the production of the means of production had a natural priority.

(4) It involved the recruitment and training, at short notice, of a primitive peasant population, entirely unused to urban life, to labour discipline and to mechanical processes.

(5) It required, owing both to its political orientation and to the technological complexity of modern industry, a substantial element of central direction and organization.

Following the dismissal of Witte, the disaster of the Russo-Japanese War and the revolution of 1905, some of the steam went out of the process. Between 1906 and 1914 industrialization in Russia proceeded at a substantially slower rate than in the 1890s;

foreign loans and state financing of industrialization declined; the banks grew more powerful, and to some extent replaced the state as dispensers of long-term credit to industry. In Gerschenkron's analysis, this represented a certain 'westernization' or 'Germanization' of Russian industrialization (and hence an advance), under which 'the mode of substitution tended to approximate the pattern prevailing in Central Europe'. It was no longer the state, but the banks, which were 'a substitute for an autonomous internal market'. Gerschenkron regards this as a 'continuation of growth in changed conditions', showing 'elements of relaxation and "normalization" in the industrial process'. He believes that 'industry may have been passing at this time through a period of dynamic preparation for another great spurt', which 'of course never materialized' (pp. 135–7, 142). He implies, without actually saying it, that industrialization in Russia might, given time, have reverted not merely to the intermediate German, but to the basic British, model: this would have constituted the maximum of 'relaxation and "normalization" in the industrial process'. It is probably correct that between 1906 and 1914 Russian industrialization came nearer than at any other time to the pattern of industrialization of western countries industrialized with the aid of private foreign capital. It is also true that industrialization in this period attained a lower rate of growth than in the 1890s when state capital was more actively engaged and state intervention continuous, and that it owed much of such impetus as it had to the achievement of the earlier period.

But this is only half the story. The conditions of Russian industrialization, though in some respects – notably in the primitive technical and social organization of Russian agriculture – more backward than those in which English or German industrialization has taken place, were in other respects more advanced. When Russia industrialized, the age of the large-scale factory unit, of machine production and of the conveyor belt was already well on the way. The demands of this type of industry were fundamentally different, both materially and psychologically, from those of the earlier industrial revolutions. It may be that the peasant recruited into a rapidly expanding Russian industry was more 'backward' than his English predecessor. But the industry into which he was recruited was more 'advanced'. The second factor was perhaps more decisive for the course of development than the first. The discussion seems to be obscured rather than facilitated by the introduction of such concepts as 'advanced' and 'backward', or 'norms' and 'deviations'.

It is against this complex background that the history of industrialization in the Soviet Union has to be traced. The main issues of Soviet industrialization, or of a resumption of pre-revolutionary programmes of industrialization, remained latent for almost ten years after the revolution. Revolution and civil war damaged factories, destroyed machines, and dispersed the labour force. In 1922, after the introduction of NEP, Soviet industry touched its lowest point. Thereafter recovery was rapid, and by the end of 1926 production in general was back to its pre-revolutionary level. This 'restoration period' presented few problems of policy. The overriding aim was to bring factories and machines back into use and to reassemble a labour force. Demand exceeded supply; and almost everything that could be produced found an eager market. Owing to wholesale damage to blast furnaces in the Ukraine, and the catastrophic fall in the production of pig iron, metal industries lagged behind the rest. The fourteenth party conference in April 1925 sanctioned an investment programme to revive them. But this implied no special emphasis on heavy industry or on the production of capital goods. The Red Army had been demobilized and military expenditure cut to the bone; and no great works of construction were undertaken at this time. At the conference which adopted the resolution, Dzerzhinsky explained that 'the fundamental base of our metal industry as a whole . . . is the consumer market'; it was there that 'the whole strength and future of our metal industry is to be found'.[1] What was afterwards invoked as a Marxist 'law' of the priority of the production of means of production over the production of goods for consumption had no place in Soviet theory or practice in this period. The

[1] *Izbrannye Proizvedeniya* (1957) ii 83–4.

'special conference on the restoration of fixed capital in industry' (OSVOK), which was set up by Vesenkha early in 1925, and issued a number of reports in this and the following year, showed no preference for capital goods industries. Throughout this time, the only consistent advocates of industrialization in the later sense of the term were Trotsky and his followers, together with the economist Preobrazhensky, whose famous essay on 'Primitive Socialist Accumulation' dated from the autumn of 1924.

By the end of 1925 it became clear that the 'restoration period' was nearing its end, and that major decisions of policy would shortly be called for. It was freely pointed out that industry could not be expected to maintain the rate of growth of the past four years once existing means of production had been rehabilitated and brought back into use. Henceforth the rate of growth in industry would depend on decisions how much to invest and in what to invest. The new mood was registered in the resolution of the fourteenth party congress in December 1925, which bound the party to 'pursue a policy aimed at the industrialization of the country, the development of the production of means of production, and the formation of reserves for economic manœuvre'. But the decision of principle was subject to a variety of interpretations, and, in particular, said nothing about the rate of industrialization. Bukharin at the congress had consoled himself, and the more cautious among his hearers, with the admission that 'we shall move forward at a snail's pace'; and a few months later Stalin compared the ambitious Dnieprostroi project with the perversity of the peasant who neglects the repair of his plough in order to buy a gramophone. Progress was made. Even the Dnieprostroi plan, which made sense only on the prospect of an indefinitely expanding demand for power from newly created industries, was approved in the autumn of 1926. Two other major construction projects approved in 1927 were geared to agricultural policy – the Turksib railway, whose main purpose was to carry Siberian grain to the cotton-growing regions of central Asia, and the Stalingrad tractor factory. Generally speaking, the assumption prevailed that industrialization would proceed at a tempo, and in conditions, which did not involve unduly serious pressures on the peasant or on the industrial worker. A latent incompatibility between the principles of NEP and the principles of planning was only dimly perceived.

This period of compromise, wishful thinking and evasion of the real issue ended in 1927. In the summer of that year, food shortages occurred in the large cities – showing that a policy of mild appeasement of the peasant, unsupported by mass production of consumer goods, did not suffice to guarantee grain supplies; official prices for important commodities could not be held, or led to a wide divergence between these prices and free market prices – showing the impossibility of combining reliance on the market with extensive price regulation; and currency inflation could no longer be concealed – showing that financial orthodoxy was not strong enough to resist pressures on it. The crisis, accentuated by the failure of the grain collections in the last months of 1927, made some shift in policy inevitable. The choice was, broadly speaking, between two courses. Industrialization could be stepped up, reliance on the market abandoned in favour of systematic planning, and more emphasis placed on the production of capital goods as a prelude to more intensive industrialization. This was what the opposition demanded. Or the tempo of industrialization could be reduced, and the emphasis transferred to the production of consumer goods for the market. This was the line more or less openly preached, though with some cautious reservations, by Bukharin and Rykov, and widely supported in the party; on the record of the past two years, it seemed the most likely line for the party to take. In fact, once the opposition had been expelled at the fifteenth party congress in December 1927, Bukharin and Rykov were branded as heretics, and policies of rapid industrialization, with emphasis on the production of capital goods, more vigorous and intensive than the opposition had ever dared to contemplate, were adopted. The central problem of Soviet industrialization is how this came about.

The pace of industrialization seems to have been determined mainly by two contributory factors. One was the war scare in the summer of 1927 following the breaking-off of relations by Great Britain in May of that year. This was said to have aggravated the shortage of supplies by encouraging hoarding; and for the first time for many years it concentrated attention on military defence. The needs of rearmament stimulated, or reinforced, the case for the rapid development of heavy industry. Lenin had proclaimed not only that heavy industry was 'a fundamental basis of socialism', but that without it 'we shall perish altogether as an independent country'.[1] Historians with a liking for the might-have-beens of history may wish to speculate whether the tempo of industrialization would have been slower if the Soviet leaders had not in 1927 felt themselves isolated in a hostile world; or alternatively what, if the tempo had been slower, would have happened to the Soviet Union in 1941. These speculations are not particularly profitable. But the security motive in the drive to catch up with the west by rapid industrialization should not be overlooked.

The second factor was the increasing weight of unemployment. Unemployment was a difficult category to define precisely in Soviet conditions. Though an urban phenomenon, its main source was rural over-population. In the middle 1920s the Soviet Union, having recovered with extraordinary rapidity from the casualties of war and civil war, was in the midst of a 'population explosion' which was increasing the population at the rate of 2·2 per cent per annum; and this resulted in a steady influx of peasants into the towns for unskilled seasonal work, especially in building. (Rural population was increasing only by 1·6 per cent per annum, urban population by 5·1 per cent.) Some of the unemployed had no experience of wage-earning beyond a few weeks of casual labour. Statistics kept independently by the trade unions and by Narkomtrud varied widely. Both sets were incomplete, but both in 1927 returned a total of well over a million unemployed; and the opposition estimate of two millions was not unreasonable. The existence of this large untapped source of energy naturally invited the view that it should be put to work in ways which would

[1] For these quotations see *Polnoe Sobranie Sochinenii*, 5th ed. xlv 209, 287.

increase the national wealth and power. The creation of new
industrial enterprises seemed the only, though long-term, solution for an intractable problem. To increase production was the
only way to take care of an expanding population. In the controversy about Soviet industrialization, most western critics have
found themselves on the side of Bukharin and Rykov, some on
humanitarian, some on economic, grounds (the two not being
always clearly distinguished). But it has not been fashionable to
speculate what would have happened to the rural population if a
lower rate of industrialization had been adopted. The example of
India does not suggest that Bukharin's policy of 'snail's-pace'
industrialization, and avoidance of undue pressures on the peasant
or the worker, would necessarily have solved the population
problem. The Gosplan economist Bazarov once predicted that, if
agriculture were reconstructed and the countryside flooded with
consumer goods, there would be no way out but to spend on aid
to the surplus population not hundreds of millions, but milliards,
of roubles.[1] Such speculations and comparisons do not, however,
lead any further than others canvassed in this essay; and I think
that we need to take a rather more detached look at the aims and
methods of Soviet industrialization in a wider context.

A well-known work on industrialization, which was originally
published in Germany in 1931 (an English version appeared in
1958), and made no attempt to discuss Soviet industrialization,[2]
distinguished three phases through which countries commonly
pass in the course of their industrialization. The first, or initial,
phase is marked by the predominance of consumer goods industries. In the second phase capital goods industries advance rapidly,
and may approach half the output of consumer goods industries.
In the third phase, the output of capital goods industries equals
that of consumer-goods industries with a tendency on the part

[1] *Planovoe Khozyaistvo*, 1928, no. 2, p. 45.
[2] W. G. Hoffmann, *Stadien und Typen der Industrialisierung* (Kiel, 1931); *The
Growth of Industrial Economies*, tr. Chaloner and Henderson (Manchester, 1958).
A perfunctory half-paragraph on Soviet industrialization on p. 100 of the
English version was evidently an addition, since it referred to works published
in the 1950s.

of the former to expand still more rapidly, pointing to a fourth phase (not considered to have been reached anywhere in 1930), in which capital goods industries would outstrip consumer goods industries. The significant feature of this process has, however, been its accelerating character and the shortening of the phases, so that major industrial countries which had begun to industrialize much later than Great Britain – the United States, Germany, France, Sweden – had before the end of the nineteenth century caught up with Great Britain, and entered the third phase on equal terms with her; and these countries were joined after the First World War by Japan where industrialization did not begin before 1860. Moreover, countries where industrialization did not begin before 1890, or even before the First World War, had by the 1950s entered the third phase; Canada, Australia and South Africa were cited as examples. This rapid progress was attributed partly to absence of competition from 'old-established craft industries', and partly to 'action taken by governments to foster capital goods industries'.[1]

With this picture in mind, can we try to place Soviet industrialization in the perspective of a train of events set in motion by the English industrial revolution and continuing in our own time with the industrial revolution in Asia and Africa? When industrialization began in Great Britain in the middle of the eighteenth century, manufacture was still *manu*facture. The individual entrepreneur working with a dozen or a score of 'hands' was the typical unit of production; tools and machines were of the simplest kind; the capital investment required to float such enterprises was very small. It may be true that the British economy was somewhat more advanced – in the sense of having larger resources in capital and skill – when it embarked on industrialization than the continental and Russian economies of a later date when they started on the same course. But the much more significant fact is that, in the conditions of the latter part of the eighteenth century, far smaller capital resources and less technical know-how were needed to set the process of

[1] Hoffmann, *The Growth of Industrial Economies*, pp. 80, 91–2, 100.

industrialization in motion. The problem of capital accumulation, which bedevilled the later types of industrialization, arose only in the second stage of British industrialization, when internal resources had multiplied sufficiently to cope with it. When continental Europe embarked on industrialization in the middle of the nineteenth century, the essential conditions had changed. Railway construction dominated the process. Large units of production, heavy and complicated machines and large investments of capital were the order of the day. When Russia followed the same path fifty years later, technology had made further advances, and these developments were further intensified. Hence the progression from the primitive British model of industrialization by the private entrepreneur through the more advanced continental model of financing and control by the banks to the still more advanced Russian model of financing and control by the state, already discernible in the Russian industrialization of the 1890s.

The conclusion I should like to draw is that Soviet industrialization is neither a unique phenomenon, nor a deviation from an established and accepted model, but an important stage in a process of development which began nearly two centuries ago and still looks to have a long history before it. The specific feature of Soviet industrialization is its association with a planned economy, though planning is neither so complete an innovation as is sometimes believed nor confined so exclusively to the Soviet and post-Soviet economies. This can be illustrated from the principal features of planned industrialization in the Soviet Union.

(1) The unit of planning in the modern sense is the nation, and the agent of planning is a governmental authority. Historically, national efficiency was the first motive of planned industrialization: of this Russia in the 1890s provided an early example. The planning of national economies in the First World War falls into this category. The early Soviet advocates and theorists of planning were consciously inspired by the German war economy. But, in a broader sense, national planning is simply a culmination of the long process which has replaced the individual craftsman

or trader by the small business, the small business by the large share company, and the company by the mammoth trust or combine. The national planning authority presides over a group of combines. The nation has developed as the largest, and in modern conditions most efficient, unit of economic control. Economic groups or combines of small nations are the next logical step in the process.

(2) Planning means the replacement of 'spontaneous' market controls by conscious decisions of a central authority, of 'individual' rationality by 'social' rationality. Troglodytes of *laissez-faire* maintain – or used to maintain – that social purpose is necessarily irrational. It is of course true that society is composed of individuals, and that decisions taken in the name of society may be oppressive in regard to some individuals, just as decisions taken by some individuals may be oppressive in regard to others. But once we recognize the Hobbesian state of nature as intolerable, and have ceased to believe in the automatic harmony of interests, we are compelled to accept the hypothesis, which lies at the root of planning, that major economic decisions must be taken not by individuals or groups in pursuit of their own interests, but by an organ acting in the name of society as a whole. Planned Soviet industrialization was the first explicitly to embody this principle, which is now tacitly accepted – though sometimes with grudging reservations – in all major countries.

(3) All industrialization rests on the tacit assumption that, productivity of labour being higher in industry than in agriculture, the basic criterion of the economic level of any nation is the relative weight of industry in its economy; the Marxist doctrine of the destiny of the proletariat lent special importance to this factor in the drive for Soviet industrialization. It followed from this proposition that, in any advanced programme of planned industrialization, priority would be given to the expansion of capital goods industries, which would raise productivity most rapidly. This development, as has already been shown, was also a feature in pre-Soviet industrialization; and the foreshortening of the process, bringing about this development more rapidly in

later examples of industrialization, has also been noted elsewhere. It would be meaningless to attempt to assess the relative weight of these general trends and of the impact of Marxist doctrine in hastening this development in Soviet industrialization. But this was the background of the controversy with Bukharin and Rykov on the tempo of industrialization and on the priority of capital goods and consumer goods industries.

(4) Finally, Soviet industrialization was marked by a different attitude to foreign trade, due largely to specific Russian conditions. In the process of British industrialization the export of consumer goods, and later also of capital goods, had been of crucial importance. In the later stages, Great Britain became dependent on imports of food and, like other western European countries, of many of the raw materials required by advanced industries. None of these conditions obtained in Russia. Russia was an exporter of agricultural products and was well supplied with almost all essential raw materials, and was on the other hand an importer of the products of industry, both consumer goods and especially capital goods – a state of affairs which industrialization was designed to remedy. While therefore in Great Britain foreign trade and the international division of labour was thought of as an integral part of the economy and an instrument of progress, in Russia it was a badge of inferiority and backwardness, of a situation in which Russia was an 'agrarian colony' of the industrial west. The drive for self-sufficiency was from the first very strong in Soviet industrialization, partly because it seemed to be obviously practicable, and partly because it was the only road of escape from western tutelage and dependence on the west. The fear of western hostility also made it important in military terms. Foreign trade was regarded empirically as a way of obtaining some foreign product which was for the present indispensable but which might some day be replaced by a Soviet product.

But, though a cult of self-sufficiency and a cautious attitude to foreign trade were easily explicable as a result of the Soviet environment, they also represented a general trend in modern industrialization. While it is not clear that industrialization diminishes the volume of foreign trade, it certainly alters its pattern. It is perhaps unlikely that the export of textiles will ever be resumed on the scale familiar in the nineteenth century. At the height of the industrialization crisis in the Soviet Union in the late 1920s, 85 per cent of all industrial imports were capital goods. The same pattern is likely to be followed by other industrializing nations, and will for some time provide a stimulus to the capital goods industries of the older industrial countries. But much of this process at present rests on a precarious foundation, which was never available to the Soviet Union, of 'aid' rather than trade. The future of international trade in an industrialized world is still a somewhat remote speculation. The trend towards self-sufficiency exhibited by the process of Soviet industrialization seems likely to spread: even the geographical maldistribution of raw materials is a less acute problem in the era of synthetic substitutes. A tendency for international trade to be concentrated on the most advanced and complex industrial products may perhaps be foreseen. Here too Soviet industrialization seems to illustrate a specific stage in a world-wide process of development.

VIII *Soviet Trade Unions*

THE place of trade unions in a planned economy is a topical issue of great practical as well as theoretical significance. A characteristic institution of capitalism has been called on to adapt itself, sometimes consciously, sometimes almost unconsciously, to conditions in which the trade union member works no longer for the private capitalist employer, but for the public corporation or for the employer state. The nationalization of industry, whether its effects are immediately perceived or not, is clearly bound to have profound repercussions on the role and functions of trade unions.

These repercussions are discernible even in a 'mixed' economy such as at present exists in Great Britain, and are intensified when a Labour government, itself largely elected and supported by trade union influence, is at the helm. But the repercussions can be studied in pure, almost 'laboratory', conditions when the trade unions operate in a so-called workers' state under a 'dictatorship of the proletariat'. This lends a particular colour and interest to Mr Isaac Deutscher's monograph on *Soviet Trade Unions*, published by the Royal Institute of International Affairs.[1] Mr Deutscher emphasizes the danger of drawing conclusions from the Russian trade unions and applying them uncritically to those of other countries. Russian trade unions were practically non-existent before 1905: it was only after 1917 that they acquired any kind of national organization. The weakness and lack of tradition of trade-unionism in Russia stand in sharp contrast

[1] I. Deutscher, *Soviet Trade Unions: Their Place in Soviet Labour Policy* (1950).

with the situation in, say, Great Britain or Germany; and other points of difference will be noted presently. Nevertheless, any attempt to answer the crucial question where the trade unions stand, or for what they stand, in the world today will have to take account of what has been done in the Soviet Union in the past thirty years; and, owing to language barriers and other difficulties of understanding, it is valuable to have this clear and scholarly outline, achieved within a comparatively brief compass but without sacrifice of any of the points of principle, of the history of the Soviet trade unions.

The dilemma of trade unions under socialism is dimly foreshadowed in the earlier history of Marxism. The Marxist programme in its entirety constituted what could be described as a 'labour' policy. It drew the logical consequences from the theory that labour is the sole source of value; and it made the industrial proletariat both the artificer and the main beneficiary of the coming revolution. It could not disinterest itself in the demands which were the staple of trade union platforms under capitalism – higher wages, the eight-hour day and so forth. But these demands presupposed the existence of the capitalist system, and could be only secondary features in a revolutionary programme. The main purpose of the workers must be to overthrow capitalism, not to improve their own position within it. The items which figured as minimum demands of the workers in the *Communist Manifesto*, and in later party programmes inspired by it, were important not so much for their own sake, but as stepping-stones to the revolutionary goal.

This attitude was responsible for the somewhat sceptical mistrust of the trade unions displayed by early Marxists. The First International had to pick its way delicately between those of its members (mainly the English group) who thought trade-unionism the all-important form of organized labour activity and those (mainly French and German) who were inclined to dismiss it as irrelevant, if not prejudicial, to the revolutionary struggle and to the future of socialism. A resolution passed by the Geneva congress in 1866 recognized that trade unions were necessary and vital 'so long as capitalism exists', but warned them against the pursuit of 'narrow' aims and urged them to 'strive for the general liberation of the oppressed millions of working people'. What happened when parties concentrated exclusively or mainly on trade union work and trade union demands was shown by the example of the 'revisionists' in the German Social-Democratic Party in the 1890s and of the 'Economist' group among the Russian Social-Democrats a little later: the revolutionary parts of the programme were relegated to the background and the party was invited to become 'reformist' rather than revolutionary. This experience was reflected in the habit of Lenin and other Bolshevik writers of using the word 'trade-unionism' (in English) in a pejorative sense. Lenin, in 1902, in *What is to be Done?* attacked the 'Economists' for 'lapsing from social-democracy into trade-unionism', and argued that 'the political struggle of social democracy is far broader and more complex than the economic struggle of the workers with the employers'. He even thought at this time – though he soon changed his view – that trade unions should be encouraged to remain politically neutral and that social-democrats should not seek to win control of them.

The Bolshevik attitude to trade unions was theoretical so long as Russian unions were still non-existent or embryonic. Before 1905 the strikes which occurred in Russian factories were almost entirely unorganized, and represented little more than spontaneous outbursts of revolt against intolerable hardships. In 1905 the trade unions received their first great impetus to grow. But even at this moment they were eclipsed, as organs of the recalcitrant workers, by the Soviets – a novel and specifically Russian form of organization which had from the first a political and revolutionary complexion. In the period of repression after 1906 the trade unions suffered almost complete extinction; and when they revived and spread after the February revolution of 1917 they were once more overshadowed in the consciousness of the most active and radical workers by the prestige of the Soviets; the trade unions, though they now enrolled largely increased numbers of the workers, played no role whatever in the October revolution.

Meanwhile a new rival to the trade unions had appeared on the scene in the form of factory committees which, having spread spontaneously through the factories after the February revolution, received legal recognition under the Provisional Government as entitled to represent the workers in their relations to the employer. These committees were in many respects the counterpart of the shop-stewards' organizations which a little later were to challenge the central trade union organizations of both Great Britain and Germany; but in Russia, where organized trade-unionism was still exceedingly weak, they played for a short time a much more conspicuous role. They became the embodiment of a Bolshevik slogan of 'workers' control', which meant, or was supposed to mean, not only that the workers as a whole should take over state power through the Soviets, but that individual factories should pass under the control of the workers employed in them. The situation was complicated by the fact that, while the Bolsheviks were supreme in the factory committees, the trade unions, whose membership was drawn to a larger extent from the more skilled workers' groups, were at this time often dominated by the more cautious Mensheviks.

Down to the moment of the October revolution, therefore, the Bolsheviks had every motive to support the factory committees, which, with their slogan of 'workers' control', were revolutionary in outlook and predominantly Bolshevik, rather than the trade unions, which were mainly 'reformist' and Menshevik. But the revolution, by putting the Bolsheviks in power, quickly transformed their outlook. The new government hastened to enact such measures of labour legislation as had long been familiar in western democratic countries, though without much regard to their practicability in existing Russian conditions – the eight-hour day, compulsory rest days and holidays with pay, restriction on work of women and juveniles, prohibition on employment of children under 14. Provision was made for social insurance against sickness and unemployment and its administration entrusted, in default of any other convenient organ, to the trade unions. On the other hand, the initial legislation on 'workers' control' quickly broke down, leading to anarchy in the factories and a catastrophic decline in production, largely because of the total inability of the factory committees to take the place of the managerial and technical staffs who, not unnaturally, refused to operate the new system.

This situation brought about a complete, though gradual, reversal of the old attitude towards the trade unions. On the one hand, the new regime clearly needed some recognized central organization representative of labour interests if its industrial policy was to be made to work at all. On the other hand, the trade union movement was clearly likely to relapse into insignificance if it failed to make its terms with the government. The turning-point was marked by a first All-Russian Congress of Trade Unions which met at Petrograd in January 1918, and, for the first time at any representative trade-union assembly, showed a Bolshevik majority. It was this congress which proclaimed, with a certain discreet vagueness about the time-table, that the trade unions would 'inevitably be transformed into organs of the socialist State' and that workers' membership of the unions would be 'part of their duty to the State'.

From this time forward the doctrine of the integration of the trade unions into the state machine was no longer seriously contested. The unions not only assumed, or claimed, the role of organizing production and allocating the labour force, but played an important part in the mobilization of man-power for the civil war. It was the civil war and the rigid economic system which accompanied it – known to subsequent writers under the name of 'war communism' – which introduced the forced mobilization of workers into 'labour armies', the branding of absenteeism as 'labour desertion' and the institution of a labour discipline whose enforcement was accepted by the trade unions as part of their natural task. Though these specific conditions were reversed when NEP was introduced in 1921, they left a certain mark on later developments; the trade unions never entirely liberated themselves from the role of agents of the state for the mobilization and regimentation of labour which they had accepted during the civil war.

When the civil war finally ended in the late autumn of 1920 and the stage was set for the coming of NEP, a violent controversy flared up in the party over the status of the trade unions. Trotsky, exploiting to the full the old Bolshevik prejudices against 'trade-unionism', wanted the formal incorporation of the unions in the state. On the opposite wing a group of old trade unionists and others of syndicalist leanings (the 'workers' control' movement in the early days of the revolution had had a distinct syndicalist flavour) came out for the control of industry by trade unions independent of the state. Lenin took an intermediate position which finally won acceptance in the party but proved a rather indeterminate compromise: the trade unions were to remain as an autonomous entity to protect the interests of the workers, but were at the same time to regard the stimulation of production as their main function.

The introduction of NEP, which meant the partial restoration of a capitalist economy, should in theory have helped the trade unions to regain a part of the independence which they naturally enjoy under a capitalist system. That this did not happen was due to two causes. In the first place the large-scale industries in which the vast majority of trade unionists were employed remained for the most part under state ownership even in the heyday of NEP: these were, in Lenin's phrase, the 'commanding heights' of the economy which the state must at all costs continue to hold. Secondly, the party had by this time secured the same undisputed control over the trade unions which it exercised over the organs of the state; the formal relations between the state and the trade unions ceased to be a significant issue, nor could any real clashes occur between them, when both took their orders from the same source. But in a significant document of the period Lenin listed the contradictions inherent in the position of the trade unions – the contradiction between the usual trade union method of persuasion and education of its members and the occasional acts of compulsion to which trade unions had to resort in their capacity as 'sharers of the State power'; the contradiction between the defence of the workers' interests and the 'pressure' which they had to exercise in the interests of the national economy as a whole; the contradiction between the method of bargaining and conciliation and the rigours of class warfare which could not always be avoided so long as NEP encouraged the continued existence of a capitalist class.

Both the position of the trade unions in Soviet Russia and the theoretical justification of that position had been established before Lenin died. The developments that came after proceeded logically from the premises laid down in these early years of the revolution; and Mr Deutscher has been right to devote half of the limited space at his disposal to this period. The debates that preceded the introduction of the first five-year plan in 1928 were the last occasion on which Tomsky voiced what may be called an independent trade union view. The trade union leadership by this time had moved far over to the Right wing of the party – a phenomenon not unknown in other countries – and regarded with mistrust the intensification of industrial development which was the essence of the plan. This was not surprising. The large body of unemployed who would be absorbed by the plan were not in the trade unions and had no influence on their policy: many of the workers in employment feared the 'dilution' and consequent inroads on their position which further industrialization might bring: the trade-union leaders may have foreseen that, under planning, the last vestige of their freedom of action would disappear. The adoption of the plan meant the displacement of Tomsky, who was succeeded by the more pliable Shvernik, and the resumption of policies of recruitment reminiscent of the days of 'war communism'. By 1930 the slack of unemployment had been wholly taken up and conditions established for a wholehearted and ruthless direction of labour through the trade unions, which has not since been relaxed, though conscription of labour was not formally enacted till after the outbreak of war in 1941.

The Soviet trade unions, having begun by accepting the premise that their primary function was to stimulate production, thus logically passed into the position of agents for the distribution and deployment of the labour force, and finally, as Mr Deutscher puts it, of 'recruiting agents for the industrial management'. By the 1930s the trade unions had long ceased to have any independence as against the state, which was also the employer. This did not, however, mean that they had no function to fulfil, provided that one does not seek to identify their function with that of trade unions under capitalism. They protected the interests of labour in the same way, and in the same degree, in which departments of government may normally be said to look after the particular interests of the particular sector of the economy with which they are concerned. The trade unions are consulted in the framing of the five-year plans and of the plans subsidiary to them. They thus have a voice not only in fixing the planned norms of production but also in deciding what proportion of the national production is to be devoted to consumer goods; and it is this proportion which, in a planned economy, places a *de facto* ceiling over the total wages bill, though the distribution of wages between different categories of workers still remains open to adjustment.

Other functions are of more direct and immediate importance to the individual worker. The mass transfer of workers from the country to the factories, which is the human side of 'industrialization', has always in history been a rough and callous process. After the shocking brutalities of collectivization in the early 1930s, the trade unions have done something, by training and housing schemes (often better in conception than in execution) and by the administration of social services and factory inspection, to organize and ease the difficult transition. The whole of the social services and other prerogatives of the People's Commissariat of Labour were handed over to the trade unions as long ago as 1933. Nevertheless, the power and the willingness of the trade unions and the factory committees to intervene in questions of management in defence of the workers have steadily diminished since the 1920s; and the gap between the trade union leadership and the rank and file of trade union members – a phenomenon which has also attracted increasing attention in other countries – has grown steadily wider. Mr Deutscher shows that at the tenth All-Russian Trade Union Congress in 1949, the only one held since 1932, less than a quarter of the delegates were workers, and 43 per cent full-time trade union officials. In the USSR, even more conspicuously than elsewhere, the spontaneous element in the trade union movement tends to be stifled by an all-powerful trade union bureaucracy.

But the basic issue underlying all the others is the question of compulsion. By the middle 1930s the Soviet Government had established what was in fact a system of compulsory direction of labour organized and enforced through the trade unions. This system was riveted on the country by the cruel experience of the Second World War; and, in spite of some formal mitigations, it does not seem to have changed in substance since. Thus the ultimate outcome has been a 'militarization of labour' on the lines advocated by Trotsky in 1920 under the pressure of the civil war and 'war communism'.

Trotsky would have been on stronger ground if he had been content to preach compulsory labour service as a temporary concession to military emergency. He did not do this. He supported his proposals with the familiar Marxist argument of the illusory nature of freedom – as applied to 'free' labour – under the capitalist system, and proceeded not only to maintain that all labour was compulsory (which in a certain abstract sense is true) but to attack as a 'wretched and miserable liberal prejudice' the belief that labour under crude forms of serfdom is less productive than the relatively 'free' labour of the capitalist system. Mr Deutscher points out that, from the standpoint of Marx, the 'free' forms of capitalist labour, though illusory when judged by the real freedom of a hypothetical socialist order, represented a real progress against the naked compulsion of slavery or serfdom, a relapse into which would therefore be wholly retrogressive and reactionary. Incidentally, Trotsky, by the position which he took up in 1920, deprived himself of every shred of consistency when he afterwards assailed the Stalinist labour policy.

The last chapter of Mr Deutscher's book is devoted to the question which is bound to occur to every western reader: how far the compulsory direction of labour is inherent in a planned economy and how far Soviet precedents apply to western conditions. That some planning of labour is an essential constituent part of any economic planning is plain enough. But, as Mr Deutscher observes, 'the amount of direction of labour introduced in wartime Britain' could scarcely be represented in good faith as even the embryonic form of a return to serfdom, and in fact 'did not seem to the working classes to be as oppressive as the uncertainty and misery of the booms and slumps of the preceding era'. A certain amount of planning and compulsory direction of labour is the price that has to be paid for full and stable employment; and the more straightforwardly this elementary truth is faced by the workers and by their trade unions, the less difficult and less oppressive the practical application of the principles is likely to be. If this is one of the lessons that can be learned from the story of the Soviet trade unions, it is sound and salutary.

But if this means either that the Soviet precedent offers in detail an example for imitation, or that Soviet policies concerning the status of labour or of the trade unions are imposed by the necessities of any planned economy, the conclusion will not withstand examination. In the first place Soviet policies were built on a tradition and on conditions utterly alien to those of the west. The trade unions had no inherent strength and could appeal to no deep-seated loyalties in the workers themselves; if they were to act, they had often to act by methods of compulsion simply because the confidence they enjoyed and the powers of persuasion at their disposal were so limited. In the partnership between trade union organs and those of the state the struggle was too unequal. The trade unions were in a position of hopeless inferiority from the start. More important still, the status and experience of the Russian worker divided him sharply from the workers in the old and highly developed capitalist countries. The Russian worker was at best only one generation removed from the peasant. Most often, he had started life in a peasant family; it was still by no means unusual for him to return to the country to work in the harvest; unemployment in industry meant that he resumed his former peasant status. Thus the Soviet industrial worker had no habit or tradition of factory discipline, of the life-long acquisition of industrial skills, or of voluntary combination in disciplined trade unions or factory organizations. To indus-trialize Soviet Russia it was not enough to build factories and instal machines; it was necessary also to mould peasants into industrial workers.

Secondly, whereas the old socialist writers, Marx included, had always looked forward to the future socialist order as a regime of abundance building on the foundations of a fully matured capital-ism, the planned Soviet economy has from the outset had to operate in conditions of extreme poverty and scarcity. It is true that relative scarcities have provided the main impetus to plan-ning in western countries, and that planning has then incurred some of the odium which results from its association with short rations. But the scarcity of the west would at any period have seemed abundance in Russia; and it is impossible to understand the harsh necessities of the Russian planned economy unless the extreme penury of the country at the moment when it embarked on the experiment is taken into account. This is not to condone many of the methods actually employed: some of these arose out of other aspects of the Russian political tradition and not at all from the economic necessity of planning. There is sufficient ground here, as Mr Deutscher shows in his last chapter, to resist any rash deductions from Soviet to western conditions. This is an illuminating study both of the Soviet trade unions and of the fundamental problems of trade-unionism in a period when the conditions of its origin and growth have begun everywhere to crumble. But the Soviet experience need not be treated either as a beacon to guide or as a scarecrow to deter.

IX *The Tragedy of Trotsky*

(i) THE VICTOR

OF the three giant figures looming up out of the landscape of the Russian revolution, Trotsky is the most dominant and the most dramatic. Both Lenin and Stalin in their different ways may be said, on a considered view, to have made greater contributions to history. But both subdued their personalities to the colour and shape of the revolution, immersed themselves in it, and became a part of the historical events which are associated with their names, so that their biographies can be little else than a section of the history of their times. Trotsky wrote more often and more eloquently than either of them of the role of the individual as the agent of a History which he loved to personify. But the career of Trotsky reveals far more of the individual, of the eccentric, of the unaccountable. His personality is more sharp-edged, more self-contradictory, more intriguing – in a sense, even, more endearing in its qualities and in its defects – than that of either of his partners, or rivals, in the great enterprise of the Russian revolution. It was this vivid quality which made Trotsky, by common consent, a very great orator. Even in the medium of the written word his brilliant, sometimes too rhetorical, style outshone the matter-of-fact prose of the other leaders of the revolution.

All this goes to show that Trotsky is an unrivalled subject for biography. Mr Deutscher's *The Prophet Armed*[1] is a more penetrating and more mature work than his earlier biography of Stalin, dramatic though that was and unsuperseded though it

[1] I. Deutscher *The Prophet Armed. Trotsky: 1879–1921* (1954).

still remains. The present book has the advantage that the author, though far from uncritical, has a basic sympathy with Trotsky as marked as his antipathy for his previous subject. It is also, far more than its predecessor, a work of original research. This is the first time that use has been made on a substantial scale of the unpublished Trotsky Archives in the Houghton Library at Harvard. On the other hand, we have so far only the bare torso of the whole work. The present volume stops at 1921 with Trotsky apparently at the summit of his career and with Lenin's health and strength still unimpaired. Mr Deutscher in his preface speaks of 'the truly classical tragedy of Trotsky's life, or rather a reproduction of classical tragedy in terms of modern politics'. The tragic years still lie ahead; and the further instalment or instalments – for one will scarcely suffice if, as is greatly to be hoped, the biography is to be completed on the scale on which it has been begun – will be eagerly awaited.

The title of the volume is suggested by a passage in *The Prince*, where Machiavelli, speaking of the obstacles that confront the innovator who seeks to 'take the lead in the introduction of a new order of things', observes that 'all armed prophets have conquered, and the unarmed ones have been destroyed'. It is possible, as Mr Deutscher himself confesses, to cavil on the appositeness of the text. The victories of Bolshevism, and Trotsky's individual victories, were scarcely won by force of arms. In material resources and in armaments the odds were always on the other side; and the achievement of the revolution was that it built up its power in the face of these apparently overwhelming odds. But it is true that Trotsky appears throughout the period covered by this volume as the victorious prophet, the conquering hero. The three high spots of this part of his career are his leadership in the 1905 revolution when, at the age of twenty-six, he emerged as the dominant figure in the self-constituted Petersburg Soviet; his major role in the military preparations for the October revolution in 1917; and his organization of the Red Army in the civil war.

The role of Trotsky in the 1905 revolution was outstanding,

and had two aspects, practical and theoretical. His determination and his eloquence, both in the meetings of the Soviet and in his subsequent trial before a Tsarist court, were factors of primary importance in building up the authority and prestige of the Soviet, and in creating a revolutionary myth whose power was to be demonstrated in the culminating moment of October 1917. Both in 1905 and in 1917 it was Trotsky, not Lenin, who was the protagonist of the Soviet idea, and gave shape to a spontaneous flowering of loosely knit, democratic assemblies of industrial workers. For Trotsky, though not for Lenin, it was the Soviets rather than the party which provided his main platform. For Trotsky the Soviets from 1905 onwards were the symbol of the revolution: he became a Bolshevik only in 1917.

It was, however, Trotsky's role in 1917 which proved historically the most decisive, and which has since been subjected to the largest measure of distortion and controversy. In describing the measures and the decisions which led up to the victorious revolutionary *coup* in October, it is not easy, with the greatest impartiality in the world, to hold the balance fairly between Lenin, still in hiding and emerging from time to time to exhort and encourage the party central committee by letter or by a surreptitious visit to Petrograd, and Trotsky, president of the Petrograd Soviet and of its military-revolutionary committee, engaged, in almost open defiance of the Provisional Government, in the practical preparations for the insurrection. Nor is it surprising that between two men so differently placed with such different political backgrounds, though now inspired by an identical aim and an equally imperative sense of urgency, differences of opinion' should have arisen on such matters as dates and tactics. A few years after 1917, when memories were still green, Stalin himself paid tribute to Trotsky's role as the organizer of the revolution. Later, that role was little by little disparaged until, in modern official histories of October 1917 Trotsky is eliminated altogether from the picture, or appears only as attempting to delay or sabotage the well laid plans of Lenin and Stalin. It is not the function of Trotsky's biographer to decry the deserts of his hero. But

Mr Deutscher, who also has designs on a future biography of Lenin, picks his way along this thorny path with tact and discretion. In the achievement of the victory of October 1917, there is room both for a Lenin and for a Trotsky.

The third episode in which Trotsky's service to the revolution was pre-eminent and irreplaceable was the organization and conduct of Soviet military action in the civil war. The disintegration of the Tsarist army had been a necessary part of the revolution – not merely a casual by-product, but one of its essential aims. The inevitable consequence had been revealed in the helplessness of Soviet policy at Brest-Litovsk and of Soviet resistance to further German incursions. Trotsky boldly attacked the problem in the spring and summer of 1918 amid the first rumblings of civil war and counter-revolution. In the teeth of opposition from the military pundits of the party, who still talked in terms of partisans and militiamen under elected leadership, Trotsky set out to create the nucleus of a new, centralized Red Army, and called in the aid of former Tsarist officers to train and lead it. Step by step, he built up a force capable of meeting and defeating the raw levies of the White generals. It was a feat of organizing genius to which both Lenin, and more than one leading German general of the day, paid outspoken tribute.

In the strategy of the campaigns of the civil war Trotsky's role was less outstanding and his success more dubious. One of the notable merits of Mr Deutscher's biography is that he has for the first time, with the aid of the Trotsky Archives, disentangled the main threads of a story deliberately confused and obscured by later Stalinist recriminations. That Trotsky made mistakes, that he was more than once, rightly or wrongly, overruled, and that Lenin strove consistently to hold the uneasy balance between him and Stalin, lest he should lose the services of one or the other of these indispensable lieutenants – all this emerges clearly from the narrative. What is surprising is, perhaps, that victory should have come at all to an army whose supreme commanders were so much at loggerheads among themselves. Trotsky fairly deserves to be hailed as the victor in the civil war, but in virtue of his organizing abilities and of the inspiration which the Red Army drew from his magnetic personality in the field rather than of his direction of military operations. On the whole, it is remarkable how little foundation there was for the charge levelled against him of trying to make himself a Napoleon.

Trotsky might, on the strength of this triumphant record, have gone down in history pre-eminently as a man of action. But Trotsky was a Marxist, who believed in the unity of theory and practice; and his contributions to the theory and the historiography of the revolution were by no means the least remarkable part of his achievement. Again and again, during his rich and varied career, he wrote with extraordinary prescience of revolutionary tendencies and developments, though he did not always, when the time came, know how to turn his own analyses and predictions to account. 'Lenin's method', he wrote in 1904, in the heat of the first breach between Bolsheviks and Mensheviks after the second party congress, 'leads to this: the party organization substitutes itself for the party as a whole; then the central committee substitutes itself for the organization; and finally a single dictator substitutes himself for the central committee.' Whatever may be thought of this as a verdict on the party which Trotsky was himself to join thirteen years later, and to serve for ten years, it was an exceedingly acute observation on a development then existing only in embryo.

Trotsky's major contribution to party doctrine was the so-called theory of 'permanent revolution' – a phrase which he borrowed from Marx, but to which he gave a new and special sense designed to reflect and illuminate Russian conditions. Convinced of the bankruptcy of the Russian middle class and of its liberal politicians, the product of the over-rapid and artificial expansion of Russian industry under the dual impulse of state orders and foreign loans, Trotsky saw, earlier than any other revolutionary leader, the difficulty inherent in applying to Russia the Marxist scheme, derived from the study of western conditions, of a bourgeois revolution leading on by a natural and inevitable process to the future proletarian revolution. In Russia the bourgeoisie was not, and never would be, strong enough to make the bourgeois revolution. The experience of 1905 persuaded Trotsky that the workers would no longer wait for a revolution which did not come. In Russia, he predicted, the worker would find himself in power 'before his master', and would be compelled to complete the bourgeois and proletarian revolutions of the Marxist plan in a single continuous operation. It was the doctrine which in essence, if not in form, lay at the foundation of Lenin's famous 'April theses' of 1917, and pointed the way to the seizure of power in October.

Throughout his career Trotsky continued to have these uncannily apt premonitions of what lay ahead. As early as 1908 he accurately foresaw the hesitations about the party's future course which would overtake many – if not most – of the leading Bolsheviks when the February revolution confronted them with the concrete issue of their attitude to a so-called bourgeois government. He was the founder of the Red Army for the defence of the 'socialist fatherland'. He was the first advocate of the large-scale 'direction' of labour. He outlined NEP a year before it became practical politics. From the early 1920s onwards he was an untiring advocate of national planning, at that time regarded with cautious scepticism by every other leader – not excluding Lenin. Yet on one issue of crucial importance he was wholly mistaken; and, while his mistake was at first shared by every other Bolshevik of any account, he was the slowest of them all to abandon his illusions and to adjust his course to an unwelcome reality.

Trotsky was a passionate believer in the accepted view that the proletarian revolution, while it might break out first in Russia, would quickly spread over Europe and especially over Germany, and that, unless it did so, the Russian revolution by itself could not hope to survive. 'European war', he wrote as early as 1906, 'inevitably means European revolution.' For Trotsky the Russian revolution, except as part of a world-wide revolution, seemed meaningless and irrelevant – as Marx had once said of a revolution which did not reach England, 'a storm in a teacup'. In March 1917, conjuring up for a moment the vision of a Russian revolution which did not spread to Germany, he decided that 'we need not rack our brains over so implausible a hypothesis'. He continued to believe – it was certainly not an absurd or paradoxical conviction – that Germany missed a proletarian revolution in the winter of 1918–19 only because it lacked an organized Communist party and resolute leaders. Oddly enough, Trotsky's illusion centred almost wholly on Germany: he was one of those who opposed the attempt to carry revolution to Warsaw at the point of Soviet bayonets in the summer of 1920. But October 1923 found him once more – and for the last time – a fervent believer in the imminence of the German revolution. Trotsky's adversaries found it easy to fasten on him – in substance, unjustly – the label of revolutionary adventurism in Europe under the guise of 'permanent revolution'; and Stalin brilliantly cut the ground from under his feet with the doctrine of 'socialism in one country'.

If, however, we seek by way of anticipation, in Mr Deutscher's present volume, the premonitory symptoms of Trotsky's downfall, we shall find them not so much in this failure of his judgement on events as in the failure of his judgement on persons. Trotsky seems as a rule to have been remarkably successful in the choice of his subordinates and in winning their loyalty to himself: few deserted him even when fidelity became hazardous or fatal to their future prospects. But this was not enough. An administrator must know how to choose and manage subordinates and get the best work out of them; a politician must know how to deal with equals. Lenin, perhaps, put his finger on this spot when, in the 'testament', he criticized Trotsky as being 'too much attracted to the administrative side of affairs'. Trotsky was never wholly at ease with those whom he regarded as his intellectual inferiors, but none the less had to treat as equals. The common charge against him was one of arrogance – what Lenin more gently called 'far-reaching self-confidence'. As a politician – using the term to mark a distinction on the one hand from the administrator and on the other from the political thinker and man of ideas – Trotsky never seems to have displayed this self-confidence. In practice he too often fumbled, changed his ground (as in the

Brest-Litovsk controversy), dismayed his supporters by yielding where everyone had looked to him to stand firm, and was obstinate when obstinacy had become useless.

This weakness in the handling and the understanding of men who stood on the same level of action with himself came out strongly in his initial attitudes both to Lenin and to Stalin. Throughout the period before 1917, when Lenin was step by step winning uncontested recognition as the leader of the Bolshevik faction, Trotsky continued to treat him as a pettifogging, hair-splitting lawyer. What is significant is not that, in the heat of factional debate, he sometimes indulged in crude abuse (Lenin did the same), but that he seems to have had no conception at all of the stature of the future maker of the revolution. It is easier to understand at a later stage his contemptuous neglect of Stalin; for this view was at first the common one in the party. But as late as 1923 and 1924, when Zinoviev had begun to exhibit clear symptoms of alarm at Stalin's monopoly of authority over the party machine, and Lenin's testament had sounded an emphatic note of warning, Trotsky remained obstinately blind to the extraordinary power and acumen of the man who, in the succeeding period, was to hold the destinies of the party and of Russia in his hand.

Given Trotsky's qualities, perhaps the most remarkable feature in his whole career was the way in which, from 1917 down to Lenin's illness and death, he wholeheartedly rallied to Lenin's leadership, and bowed to decisions which he had at first uncompromisingly opposed, merely because Lenin had endorsed them. The relation in this period between two men who had unfailingly attacked and abused each other for more than ten years did credit to both; and the popular legend of 'Lenin and Trotsky' as the twin leaders of the revolution had a solid basis in fact. The deciding voice in the last resort was Lenin's – and not only because the party would listen to him, where it would not listen to Trotsky, but because of the peculiar character of the personal relation between them. Trotsky as a politician, as the sequel was to show, was helpless without Lenin, whereas for Lenin Trotsky was

merely the first of his adjutants. But, in the working out of the
partnership, Trotsky was pre-eminent in executive action, and at
times also influential in counsel. In the public eye his role seemed
even greater than it was, and, especially abroad, sometimes
eclipsed that of Lenin himself.

Mr Deutscher's first volume has shown Trotsky rising to the
peak of his achievement. His last chapter, entitled 'Defeat in
Victory', shows the hero 'stumbling' into tragedy through the
abandonment of the hope of proletarian democracy, and acceptance of the militarization of labour and of the trade unions as a
permanent aim of policy. The tragedy of Trotsky is thus equated
with the tragedy of the Bolshevik regime. The theme will doubtless be further elaborated in later chapters, and judgement on it
may for the moment be suspended. This is biography of a high
order; and even if it be true that 'good biography is necessarily
bad history', in that it concentrates the spotlight on individual
idiosyncrasies rather than on major social forces, the most austere
historian will not seek to eliminate from his pages the personal
enigma of so central a character of the Russian revolution as
Trotsky. In such a case, biography is an essential contribution to
history.

(ii) THE VANQUISHED

THE first instalment of Mr Deutscher's biography of Trotsky,
published five years ago, covered the period of his hero's ascent,
leaving him in the spring of 1921 at the pinnacle of his authority
and glory. The civil war, in the winning of which he had played
so stirring a part, was over. Lenin was at the height of his powers,
his health still unimpaired. The names of Lenin and Trotsky
were everywhere linked as the makers and heroes – or villains
– of the revolution; and their roles were felt to be equal and
complementary. They had on occasion differed in the past, and
they continued to differ. But nobody doubted the essential solidarity of the mutual confidence between them.

From this time, however, the descent began. Fresh from the
glories of the revolution and the civil war, Trotsky never fitted

easily into the pedestrian and often disheartening work of recon-struction – the struggle against want and apathy and disorganiza-tion. Lenin's first illness in the spring of 1922, and total incapacity a year later, deprived him of the solid prop on which his out-standing position in party and state had – far more than he knew – depended. Mr Deutscher's second volume covers the period of the fall, and ends with his forced departure from Russia, a hounded and discredited exile.[1]

If Trotsky's career as a whole is viewed as a tragedy – and it is certainly of tragic dimensions – this period was the heart of the tragedy. But it is a difficult period for the biographer. The hero is no longer a continuously creative figure; his biography is no longer the record of his achievement. It is the essence of Trotsky's fall that he was continuously placed on the defensive and con-demned to passivity. He was assailed unawares by forces which be-wildered him, and the strength of which he failed for a long time to recognize. He resisted half-heartedly or not at all; then, when in desperation he made a move, it turned out to be the wrong move. It is, of course, true that, in Stalin, Trotsky encountered a consummate political tactician, and that Trotsky's intellectual genius, and immense powers of administration and organization, did not include the sense of political timing, the tact in handling people and situations, which is part of the necessary equipment of every successful statesman or politician. In this sense Trotsky's tragedy can be treated as one of personal qualities and short-comings, and the issue as a mere struggle for power between unequally equipped rivals.

But Mr Deutscher is not the kind of biographer who succumbs to the temptation of reducing history to a game of mingled skill and chance, the outcome of which depends on the relative apti-tudes of the players and the luck of the cards. He is an exceedingly vivid writer with a sense of style, and a warm and understanding sympathy for his hero: this makes him a first-rate biographer. But he also has the passion for analysis of the true historian, the eternal search for the answer to the question Why? And his

[1] I. Deutscher, *The Prophet Unarmed. Trotsky: 1921–29* (1959).

answers are always based on wide knowledge and acute observation. In his story of Trotsky's life, personal, political and economic factors are woven together. The biography of the man becomes an analysis of the society.

Trotsky's biography in this period falls into three sections. In the first he gradually drifts, even before Lenin's final stroke, into a position of isolation from the ruling group. Mr Deutscher makes much of his refusal of an offer by Lenin in 1922, twice repeated, that he should be appointed a vice-president of Sovmarkom, and conjectures that this gesture was designed by Lenin to mark out Trotsky as his principal lieutenant and to counterbalance the appointment of Stalin as general secretary of the party. The conjecture is not altogether convincing. The notion of balancing a state appointment against a party appointment seems uncharacteristic; and, if Lenin had wished to find a way of enhancing Trotsky's authority as his 'second in command', he would not have proposed merely to make him one of the three or four vice-presidents. Indeed, it is fairly clear that Trotsky's firm rejection of the plan was due to unwillingness to be placed on the same footing as Rykov, Tsyurupa and Kamenev. But the refusal increased the distance between him and the other leaders, and made it easier, when Lenin was finally removed from the scene by his last illness, for Zinoviev, Kamenev and Stalin to form a triumvirate which excluded Trotsky. From this point the triumvirate, by tactics of alternate goading and cajolery, further isolated Trotsky not only from themselves but from his potential supporters. By January 1925, he was a defeated man, deprived of his state (though not yet of his party) offices, and reduced to unresisting impotence.

The second section covers the year 1925 and the first part of 1926, during which Trotsky remained politically inactive, playing the role of a loyal and submissive party member, and engaging in minor public work. Then, in the spring of 1926, he joined the now defeated opposition of Zinoviev and Kamenev, and the struggle was reopened – this time within the party. It lasted about eighteen months, during which Trotsky, his supporters and

his new allies were deposed by stages from their various party
offices and finally, at the fifteenth party congress at the end of
1927, expelled from the party itself. Zinoviev and Kamenev
recanted. Trotsky and the more stout-hearted of his followers
chose the path of exile to remote destinations in the Soviet
Union. Trotsky's home for the next year was at Alma-Ata on the
remote borders of Kazakhstan. Then, in order to remove the
danger of his becoming, even by correspondence, the focus of a
new opposition, he was deported from the country. At the end
of the volume he is on board ship at Odessa, bound for Prinkipo.

On the personal plane the tragedy of Trotsky in these years is
that, in contradistinction to the earlier period, he ceased almost
entirely to be a man of action. In the heroic days of revolution
and civil war he had been the driver; now he was the driven. In
the collisions of the next few years the initiative no longer came
from him: the battlefield, and the time to join battle, were
chosen not by him, but by his adversaries. In the autumn of 1923,
when the triumvirate launched the first campaign against him,
he allowed himself to be lured into a seeming compromise, disowned those who would have supported him, and yielded help-
lessly to his assailants. A year later the story repeated itself. It is
true that the occasion of the renewal of the struggle was the
publication of Trotsky's essay *Lessons of October*. But the record
makes it clear that it was the triumvirate which chose to treat it
as a signal for battle, not Trotsky who intended it as such. As
before, Trotsky was caught unawares and unprepared by the fury
of the attack. In both these successive autumns his health broke
down under the strain. He succumbed to a 'mysterious illness'
which defied diagnosis, and withdrew under medical advice to the
Caucasus, to re-emerge recovered when the crisis was over.

After the eighteen months' interval of inaction Trotsky resumed the struggle in June 1926, now in league with Zinoviev
and Kamenev; but, as Mr Deutscher says, 'the battle was joined
partly on Stalin's initiative'. The story of this last struggle, which
went on until November 1927, is told by Mr Deutscher with a

wealth of detail and enlightening comment. Only once or twice is one tempted to cavil at some minor point. In the midst of the debate in Moscow the full text of Lenin's famous 'testament' was published in translation in the *New York Times*. Mr Max Eastman, who was responsible for the publication, has told Mr Deutscher that he received the text from Souvarine, an oppositionist in Paris whom Trotsky had disowned, with an encouragement to publish it; and Mr Deutscher accepts as 'undoubtedly correct' the 'surmise' that the encouragement came from Trotsky. No evidence is quoted to support the conjecture. It is surely improbable that Trotsky would have been privy to the publication of the 'testament' in an American newspaper, or that he would have used Souvarine as a go-between for such a purpose. And one would like to have some evidence for the statement that Zinoviev and Kamenev 'had at the fourteenth congress raised anew the demand for the publication of the will and had repeated it at every subsequent opportunity'. It may be true; but it seems out of character.

It is symptomatic of this ill-matched struggle that, as Trotsky's position became more hopeless, his moral stature rose. In October 1926, the opposition made one more futile attempt at re-cantation and compromise, which in accordance with the precedent of Stalin's previous tactics led not, as Trotsky and Zinoviev fondly hoped, to a truce, but merely to an intensification of the assault. But this was the last of Trotsky's wanton acts of self-humiliation. In 1927 came Trotsky's appearance at the Executive of the Communist International – his last public debate against his persecutors and his first unqualified and unconditional public burning of boats – and the drawing up of 'the platform of the opposition', which quickly became a banned document circulating clandestinely. In the final crisis, with Zinoviev and Kamenev once more taking the path of recantation, Trotsky stood firm and defiant, denouncing the argument which he had used over and over again in the past three years, and which had frustrated all his activity, that 'one cannot be right against the Party'. He now boldly claimed to be 'right against the Party'. At the moment when he was about to be deprived of all freedom of action, he regained his freedom of thought.

The year spent at Alma-Ata, in remote and uncomfortable seclusion, was therefore for Trotsky a period of stocktaking and, in a sense, of rehabilitation and self-justification. In endless correspondence with other members of the opposition in exile in other parts of eastern Russia and Siberia – notably with Rakovsky, Preobrazhensky and Radek – he could assert without equivocation the positions which he had failed to defend consistently during the troubled years in Moscow. The correspondence has its moments of futility. Under the harsh condition of exile and isolation the opposition begins to crumble, and is divided by arguments which provide a first foretaste of the scholastic disputations between different sects of Trotskyites which were to mark the 1930s. But, by and large, the letters of the Alma-Ata period – now revealed for the first time from the rich storehouse of the Trotsky Archives in Harvard – are fine examples of Trotsky's powerful intelligence, at grips, without the compromises and inhibitions of the middle 1920s, with the baffling problems of the revolution. By the same token, this is rewarding ground for the biographer. Mr Deutscher's concluding chapter is the most compact and persuasive, as well as the most original, in the book. Drawing on the unpublished material of the archives, he has given a memorable analysis of the dilemma of Trotsky and of the revolution.

The essence of the dilemma, as of every problem of the Russian revolution, resides in the incongruity between its programme and the means available to carry it out. The programme of the Bolsheviks included the industrialization and democratization of Russia (which elsewhere had been the work of the bourgeois or liberal revolution) as the prelude to the creation of a new society on the basis of a socialist economy and socialist democracy (which had not yet been achieved anywhere else); the weakness of the bourgeoisie and the bankruptcy of liberalism in Russia had led to a telescoping of the two processes. The revolution itself was brought about by the action of the Petrograd industrial workers, partly spontaneous, partly organized by the small, but ably led,

Bolshevik Party; its success, however, would have been no more than momentary had not Lenin hastened to link its fortunes with the land hunger of the peasant by adding a confiscatory redistribution of the land to its programme.

But this was only the beginning of the difficulties. The virtual collapse of the economy and the administration under the stress of war and the universal loss of confidence rendered the seizure of power easier, but the exercise of power infinitely more arduous. The civil war, reinforced by foreign intervention, completed the process of disintegration. How in these circumstances was 'the dictatorship of the proletariat' or 'the workers' state' to function and to maintain itself? The early Bolshevik leaders, Lenin and Trotsky foremost among them, had only one answer. They invoked the *deus ex machina* of world revolution. The proletariats of more advanced industrial countries would make their revolutions and come to the aid of their struggling Russian brothers. On no other hypothesis could the Russian revolution hope to survive.

By 1921 the prospect of world revolution, of European revolution, of German revolution (always thought of as the first vital link in the chain) had ebbed away. The Russian revolutionary regime had demonstrated, in face of apparently overwhelming odds, its capacity for survival. But how had it survived, and how could it continue to survive? The original weak proletariat had dwindled in the process of general economic disintegration; Petrograd, the main seat of Russian industry, was in decay. As Mr Deutscher put it in the final chapter of his earlier volume, 'the Russian working class had proved itself incapable of exercising its own dictatorship'. Yet it was unthinkable that the Bolsheviks, victorious in the revolution and in the civil war, should abdicate and confess to failure in the very moment of their victory. The Party, which had always proclaimed itself the vanguard of the working class, must continue to lead. But it would not represent – though no Bolshevik admitted this, even to himself – an existing proletariat: it would be the trustee for the proletariat of the future. The path along which the Bolshevik

Party would point the way led through industrialization to proletarian socialism.

As much as anyone Trotsky stood committed to this course. More than anyone else among the leaders he accepted industrialization as the one indispensable key. In 1903 he had vehemently denounced Lenin's acceptance of the Jacobin idea of leadership by a virtuous and enlightened minority. Now he accepted it without question and apparently without any sense of inconsistency. He wholeheartedly endorsed the measures taken by the party congress in March 1921, at Lenin's instigation – measures inspired partly by the recent fright of the Kronstadt mutiny, but also by the belief that the relaxation of the economic dictatorship under NEP, though necessary for recovery, would expose the party and the regime to new political dangers – to tighten up party discipline and to prohibit the formation of factions and groupings within the party. Throughout the next six years he was inhibited not only by his refusal 'to be right against the Party', but by his loyalty to a ban which prevented him from organizing an opposition. Nor did he ever directly challenge the legitimacy of the ban. To the end he could not combine with Democratic Centralists or Decemists – the rump of an early opposition – who specifically took issue on the principles of party organization. Trotsky during the critical period of the struggle always attacked Stalin for pursuing wrong policies, never for applying wrong principles of party discipline to enforce them.

Even in Alma-Ata, this dilemma persisted. Before the final blow Trotsky had been driven to denounce the persecution of himself and his supporters, the unscrupulous methods employed by Stalin, and 'the strangling of the Party' by Stalin's bureaucracy. But this was secondary to the fundamental attack on Stalin's policy – on his support of Chiang Kai-Shek in China, on the alliance with the British trade-union leaders represented by the Anglo-Soviet joint Trade Union Council, on 'socialism in one country', and, above all, on the toleration of the kulak. When, therefore, immediately after Trotsky's exile to Alma-Ata, Stalin opened fire on the kulaks and made it clear that he was at

variance with a Right wing of the party led by Bukharin and
Rykov, Trotsky was even more a prey to a divided mind, and the
divisions were reflected in the ranks of his supporters.

For a man with Trotsky's intellectual integrity and passion for
political analysis the question whether to fight Stalin or to support
Stalin could no longer be answered with a simple 'yes' or 'no'. If
Stalin had now come over to the policy for which the opposition
had always stood – to resist the kulak and press forward industrialization and planning, while Bukharin and Rykov continued
to defend the appeasement of the kulak, one could only lend
critical support to Stalin's 'Leftist' course. On the other hand,
one must continue to fight Stalin on the issue of freedom within
the party and proletarian democracy – whatever precise meaning
Trotsky may have attributed to these phrases. Such was the
'dual attitude' which Trotsky commended in letters to the exiled
and dispersed members of the former opposition. It was not
merely the response of what Mr Deutscher calls 'dialectical
suppleness' to an 'ambiguous situation'. It was a reflection of that
tragic incompatibility between ends and means which is the
unending problem of the statesman and of the historian. Stalin's
course was set, consciously or unconsciously, to 'root out barbarism
by barbaric means'. Trotsky passionately wanted to root out
barbarism: a modernized, westernized Russia seemed to him an
essential goal of the revolution, an essential condition of socialism.
He recoiled from the means. But he had appeared to endorse
them in the past as the only means available. And he could not
reject the goal.

These doubts and these subtleties, which were so little apt for
the framing of a practical policy, had little appeal for the mass of
oppositionists in exile. It was not only the Decemists who
clamoured for a policy of 'all or nothing' and thought that, if you
wanted to fight Stalin effectively, you must fight him on all
fronts at once and with any allies who might be available. But
there were those who took the opposite view, and hoped against
hope that Stalin's turn to the Left was a prelude to a reconciliation
with the opposition, whose help he would need in the struggle

against the Bukharinist Right. It is probable that Stalin himself toyed with this idea: such a manoeuvre would have accorded with his character and record. But in practice he proved strong enough to dispense with any large-scale amnesty of the opposition, and was content to buy off individual oppositionists, or small groups of them, on terms which at once humiliated them and bent them to his purpose.

Those exiles who in the spring of 1928 were already beginning to preach conciliation of Stalin fell into two categories. The first was represented by Preobrazhensky, always the theorist rather than the politician or man of action, the most original and acute economic thinker produced by the regime, who in 1924 had begun to analyse the doctrine of 'primitive socialist accumulation' and to demonstrate that industrialization in Russian conditions implied an 'exploitation' of the peasant economy. Preobrazhensky argued that the opposition, with its superior insight, had been the true and conscious interpreter of an historic necessity. Stalin had now yielded to this necessity, though no doubt in a distorted form. But the opposition had also erred in the past in exaggerating the danger from the Right and Stalin's personal involvement in it. Preobrazhensky wanted to seek official permission for a conference of the exiled opposition with a view to altering its policy.

Of the second category Radek was the conspicuous representative. Radek, and many others like him, not primarily thinkers or theorists, found the isolation and inaction of exile intolerably irksome; and, now that Stalin was gravitating towards the line so long preached by the opposition, they seized eagerly on the pretext to seek the way of reconciliation which would restore them to active political life. It was unthinkable that Stalin and his supporters in Moscow should succeed to the legacy of the outlawed opposition, and become the executors of their policy without them. Thus a section of the opposition was already restive in the summer of 1928, and the seeds of a future recantation had already been sown. Trotsky resisted both Preobrazhensky and Radek, and incurred the criticism of both, though he was at the same time blamed by the irreconcilables for not denouncing in terms of sufficient vigour treasonable proposals to parley with Stalin. So long as Trotsky remained in Alma-Ata and was free to correspond with his supporters, he managed to hold the exiles together, or at any rate to avoid an open break; and only some isolated defections occurred in this first year. But in October 1928 censorship descended on Trotsky's correspondence, cutting him off from his followers and them from him; and three months later the sentence of banishment from the Soviet Union was pronounced and carried out. Trotsky once more became the lone wolf, and entered on the period of his life which Mr Deutscher will narrate in a third volume, *The Prophet Outcast*.

Trotsky's subsequent career, with its intermittent and fruitless attempts to re-create a coherent opposition and to frame a coherent policy, merely emphasized the dilemma and did nothing to solve it. 'The Bolshevik monopoly of power, as established by Lenin and Trotsky [writes Mr Deutscher in conclusion] found in Stalin's monopoly both its affirmation and its negation; and each of the two antagonists now dwelt on a different aspect of the problem.' And again: 'The rule of the single faction was indeed an abuse as well as a consequence of the rule of the single party.' While Stalin introduced a Marxism distorted by 'all that was primitive and archaically semi-Asiatic in Russia', Trotsky remained faithful to 'classical Marxism', which had betrayed him only owing to 'the failures of socialism in the west'. It is none the less true that Trotsky at the outset of his career had clearly predicted what would be 'the consequence of the rule of the single party', and that he had accepted it when the time came as the indispensable means of achieving, in the given conditions, the goal of the revolution. In this sense he had committed himself to the historic necessity of Stalinism, at any rate in its initial phase.

In the end Trotsky was compelled to assert the claim not only to be right against the Party but to be right against history. Trotsky had too often felt himself the agent of history, and had condemned his fallen opponents in its name. Now history had turned against him, and Stalin could invoke it in order to consign him to discredit and oblivion. At the end of his autobiography

Trotsky quotes, with an apology for the 'slight savour of eccle-
siastical eloquence', a letter of Proudhon breathing his defiance
of 'destiny'. Mr Deutscher, with a similar apology for the undercurrent of 'subjective romanticism', takes a plunge into Nietzsche:

> If you want a biography, do not look for one with the legend:
> 'Mr. So-and-So and his times', but for one in which the title
> pages might be inscribed 'A fighter against his time.' . . . For-
> tunately, history also keeps alive for us the memory of the
> great 'fighters against history', that is, against the blind power
> of the actual.

'Fine words', says Trotsky. 'Excellent words', says Mr Deutscher.
But does not this recourse to Proudhon and Nietzsche perhaps
suggest that here is a predicament of which classical Marxism
failed to take account?

(iii) The Outcast

The third and final volume of Mr Deutscher's biography of
Trotsky, *The Prophet Outcast*, completes a remarkable monument
to one of the most remarkable historical figures of the present
century.[1] Trotsky was a man of enormous vitality and immense
versatility. He was a thinker and a man of action, an orator and a
man of letters: he was outstanding in all these capacities. He was
also a man of moods. He could be romantic and melodramatic:
he could be realistic and ruthless. To do justice to so many-sided
a hero was a heavy and exacting task for a biographer. It is
scarcely necessary, at this time of day, to say that Mr Deutscher
comes through it magnificently. The final volume confirms and
enhances the reputation which the two preceding volumes have
won for him.

The theme of the third volume, which opens with Trotsky's
expulsion from the Soviet Union at the beginning of 1929, necessarily differs somewhat from that of the first two. The first
volume brought Trotsky to the summit of his achievement and
the apex of his career. The second was a record of continuous

[1] I. Deutscher, *The Prophet Outcast. Trotsky: 1929–40* (1963).

feverish struggle and – it could be said – glorious defeat. In the third volume the man of action is reduced to defiant, and occasionally also querulous, impotence. As the last decade of his life moves on, he becomes more and more isolated. He is no longer, as in his great days, the target only of his open enemies – whether of the embattled forces of the capitalist world or of Stalinists at home. His supporters begin to fall away – some returning to the Stalinist fold, others renouncing their Marxist past and making their peace with the powers that be in the western countries. The end was tragedy, not so much through the manner of his death at the hand of an assassin as through the situation into which he had already been forced. But as in all true tragedies, the end had an element of nobility to blend with the pity and the terror.

A distinctive feature of the third volume is the use which Mr Deutscher has been able to make of the so-called 'closed section' of the Trotsky Archives. When the archives were made available to scholars in the Houghton Library at Harvard at the end of the 1940s a substantial section of correspondence with supporters, and of family and business correspondence and papers, all dating from the period of exile, were reserved – apparently as the result of a request by Trotsky himself – on the assumption that their disclosure might be compromising or embarrassing to those involved: these were to become available only in 1980. Fortunately, Mr Deutscher was able to obtain the authority of Trotsky's widow to inspect these papers. Her death, which occurred while this volume was being written, removed the only surviving person who was concerned in the purely family correspondence; and the situation had changed so radically and so rapidly since the Second World War that the political papers contained – perhaps with one or two exceptions – nothing that could not be divulged without embarrassment or offence. The result is a frank and, so far as can be judged, complete biography published in an unusually short space of time after the death of its subject.

Trotsky's relations with his second wife, who accompanied him throughout his exile and was his devoted companion to the end, were almost uniformly harmonious. Hardly anything needs to be recorded of his private life except the tragic fate of his children, involved in one way or another in the persecution inflicted on him and on all who bore his name: all of them died before him. Few new facts of consequence emerge from the papers now revealed for the first time – except, perhaps, the occasionally stormy character of his relations with his son Lyova, who defended his father's cause and transacted his father's business in Paris during the whole period of exile down to his death in enigmatic circumstances in 1938. Trotsky, whose natural impatience and impetuosity of temperament had been sharpened by his terrible sense of isolation, reacted roughly to any suspicion of delay or deficiency in the execution of orders, and broke out in reproaches which seem to have been wholly undeserved. These later caused him much remorse, but appear to have cast only a passing shadow on the natural devotion which united father and son.

The successive stations of Trotsky's pilgrimage through the years of exile – Prinkipo, France, Norway, Mexico – are recorded in detail by Mr Deutscher, and finely distinguished. Paradoxically, it was the democratic countries of western Europe where he was exposed to most direct and continuous persecution, Turkey and Mexico which proved the most tolerant and indulgent hosts. It was during the three-and-a-half-year stay in Prinkipo, isolated from the world but relatively unmolested, that he wrote his two longest and most carefully pondered and polished works – his autobiography and the *History of the Russian Revolution*. In France he was hounded from place to place, his treatment by his reluctant hosts being at the mercy of every puff of rumour or political opinion or pressure from Moscow. In Norway the same experience was repeated on a still meaner and pettier scale. Trotsky missed no opportunity – and there were many in these years – of applying his mordant eloquence to the hollow hypocrisies of bourgeois freedom and bourgeois democracy.

The contrast was, however, not entirely fair or apposite. The period spent by Trotsky in Prinkipo was the period of the great economic depression in the capitalist world and of collectivization and accelerated industrialization in the Soviet Union. The clouds were gathering fast; but the political tension and the revolutionary potentialities of the situation had not yet taken shape. The years which Trotsky spent in western Europe – from 1933 to 1936 – were years in which all the familiar political landmarks were in danger of being obliterated by the flood. Hitler was striking hammer-blows at the foundations of western democracy. France was threatened with fascism. The Soviet Union was entering the period of the great purges at home, and was at the same time stretching out hands desperately to the west through the policies of the united front.

In this turmoil Trotsky remained an isolated, enigmatic and threatening figure. He was in every conceivable way and at every conceivable level the sworn foe of Hitlerism and Hitler. Nobody denounced the Nazi seizure of power or the Nazi regime in clearer or more uncompromising terms; nobody predicted as searchingly and as accurately as Trotsky whither these things were destined to lead. But Trotsky was also the demon of Stalinist mythology; Stalin was the most formidable target of Trotsky's powerful invective, though he continued to declare his solidarity with the revolution and with the 'workers' state' on the international front. His hostility to the western democracies and to western capitalism was unremitting; no place could be found for his position in the categories of western political thought. It was no accident that he remained an outcast and an unwanted alien in the western world. Great Britain and the United States of America were at least consistent and kept their frontiers firmly closed against him.

It is also true that from the moment of Hitler's rise to power – which more or less coincided with Trotsky's move to western Europe – and, still more, from the moment when the purges were launched in Moscow, Trotsky himself found not merely silence but also non-intervention intolerable, and re-entered the political fray, issuing manifestos, rallying his supporters and finally founding the Fourth International. This seemed a logical step. As in 1919 the bankruptcy of the Second International had impelled Lenin to proceed to the creation of the Third, so the still more evident bankruptcy of the Third International seemed in the 1930s to call loudly for the foundation of a Fourth. It is hardly necessary to point out the manifold differences between the two situations. Mr Deutscher belonged at the time to a group of Polish Trotskyists which opposed the move. He criticizes it again now, and has little approval for Trotsky's attempts to organize his followers politically. Though once again the situations were not really comparable, it is tempting to reflect that, even at an earlier stage of his career, the gift for political action in the narrow meaning of the term – the sense of timing and the sense of the practicable – eluded Trotsky. His diagnosis of political situations was superb. The gestures by which he staked out his position and proclaimed his principles were magnificent. Where a task had to be performed which lay near to his heart, he performed it with unmatched energy, courage and administrative ability. The timely initiation of political action remained his Achilles' heel.

While, however, it would be absurd to deny Trotsky's greatness as a man of action, the present volume and the final stage of his career inevitably show him mainly as a thinker and a writer. The ultimate question is where to place Trotsky in the analysis of the Russian revolution and its sequel. Here Mr Deutscher and his hero are one; and the answer to the question is also the author's enunciation of his political creed. Trotsky stands as the champion of the 'classical Marxism' which was the inspiration and driving-force of the Bolshevik revolution under Lenin, but from which the revolution under Stalin tragically diverged. Trotsky, almost alone, held aloft the standard of classical Marxism during the period of eclipse. What has happened since the death of Stalin marks a partial, confused and ambiguous attempt to undo the Stalinist past and return to the true path. But this is far from complete. One day, 'though not perhaps before Stalin's ageing epigones have left the stage', Trotsky's memory will be rehabilitated in the Soviet Union. This will be the decisive symbol. 'By this act the workers' state will announce that it has at last reached maturity, broken its bureaucratic shackles, and re-embraced the classical Marxism that had been banished with Trotsky.'

The two tenets of classical Marxism to which Trotsky clung with unfailing tenacity were that the consummation of the revolution which would overthrow capitalism would be the work of the proletariat, and that the revolution would assume international dimensions and not be confined to a single country. Throughout the years of exile he continued to argue that, in spite of all abuses and perversions, the Soviet Union must still be regarded as a 'workers' state'. The polemic against Stalin's 'socialism in one country' was even more deeply rooted in his mind; and when in the 1930s he presciently foresaw a second world war in which the Soviet Union would inevitably be involved, he predicted certain defeat for the Soviet forces unless the war brought revolution to Europe, so that 'the Soviet regime would have more stability than the regime of its probable enemies'.

The immediate sequel of the war would, as Mr Deutscher says, have given little satisfaction to Trotsky's views had he lived to see it. The revolution did indeed extend its sway over eastern Europe, but as a 'revolution from above' imposed by military victory. The Chinese revolution, though achieved spontaneously and with no more than ideological inspiration from Moscow, was a peasant revolution built on the ruins of the proletarian revolutionary movement of an earlier generation. Nothing here suggests a vindication of classical Marxism in the Trotskyist sense; and even in Italy and France faint stirrings of revolution soon died away. None of this necessarily refutes Trotsky's faith in the future. 'When it is a question of the profoundest changes in economic and cultural systems, twenty-five years weigh less in history than an hour in a man's life'; and Stalin's rule may yet appear as the 'episodic relapse' which Trotsky calls it. But to assert this is an act of faith. The anti-Stalinist reaction of the past ten years is beyond doubt significant. But its signs can be read in many different ways. The same might be said of the present clash between Moscow and Peking.

That these problems are posed by Trotsky's career and by Trotsky's writings in a manner which cannot be evaded is a tribute to his greatness. Even with our present incomplete perspective it would be rash to deny that the course of events set in motion by the revolution of 1917 (in so far as a precise date can be assigned to the beginning of anything in history) has set the determining pattern of history in the present century. But the critical and uncommitted historian may still wish to re-examine the concept of 'classical Marxism', and, while fully admitting the validity of much of the Marxist analysis and the vital part which it played in the Russian revolution, to inquire how far the Stalinist episode can be adequately interpreted as a 'relapse' from this concept, or the future of the revolution sought in a return to it.

Classical Marxism now has a hundred years of history behind it, and was sixty or seventy years old when it served, in its Leninist incarnation, to kindle the flames of revolution in 1917. But the revolution occurred in a country to which Marx would never have assigned the role of revolutionary leadership, with a working class far weaker and less developed than the kind of 'class-conscious proletariat' whose dictatorship he had confidently envisaged, and in economic conditions diverging widely from those of the heyday of entrepreneurial capitalism in which Marx wrote. Neither the validity of Marx's insights into the economic and political process nor their applicability to the Russian revolution will be contested. But it would have been an astonishing anomaly if that revolution, far removed in time and space from anything that Marx knew, had conformed in detail to the prescriptions of classical Marxism. To say that it did not is not to belittle Marx. But to attribute this lack of conformity to an 'episodic relapse', which began with Stalin and could be expected to end with him, seems a dangerously unhistorical approach not easy to reconcile with Marxism itself.

Historians who (like Trotsky and like Mr Deutscher) take their history seriously are apt to tie themselves in knots if they succumb to the lure of historical might-have-beens. Mr Deutscher takes

Trotsky to task for having written in his *History of the Russian Revolution* (and repeated even more categorically elsewhere) that, if Lenin had not succeeded in returning to Russia in 1917, the golden opportunity of revolution might have been let slip 'for many years'. But, not content to treat this *obiter dictum* as hollow or meaningless, Mr Deutscher is apparently eager to assert the contrary proposition: he quotes with approval Plekhanov's observation that, if Robespierre had been killed by a falling brick in January 1793, somebody else would have replaced him and subsequent events would have taken the same course. But is not this tantamount to saying that, if Stalin had been accidentally killed or had been removed after Lenin's death from his post as general secretary of the party, much the same things would have occurred under some other leader, and that what we know as 'Stalinism' was inherent in the historical situation? And from this we should apparently have to deduce that Stalinism was no mere accidental or episodic relapse from the Marxist line, but that the historical process had given the lie to 'classical Marxism'.

The historian can afford to dispense with the tortuous scholasticism which results from such excursions into the world of fantasy. The sequel of the Russian revolution was exceedingly complex. The aims and principles of the leaders rooted in Marxism, the legacy of the Russian past, the economic conditions of the present, all played important and sometimes conflicting parts in shaping the solutions which ultimately emerged. The historian will strive to disentangle the different strands, and to sort out the casual from the significant. But his standard of significance can emerge only from the process of analysis: it cannot be dogmatically derived from positions taken up in very different conditions in the past. 'Revisionism' has been a smear-word for more than one generation of Marxists: it has served too often as a cover for those who wished to retreat altogether from Marxism – or from positive action. But the time seems ripe for a searching re-examination of some of the postulates of Marxism in the light of the experience of the twentieth century, in order not to abandon the insights which it has conferred but to deepen and extend them.

The tragedy of Trotsky, from this point of view, was the tragedy of a 'classical' Marxist adrift in a world in which classical Marxism was no longer enough.

It is the merit of Mr Deutscher's book that it raises these crucial problems of the world today. This final volume of the trilogy finds its hero deprived of every means of effective action; and its character necessarily reflects the change. When the theme warrants it – Trotsky's successive journeys as a hunted exile from refuge to temporary refuge, the plots against his family and followers, the preparations for the assassination – the style is as vivid and dramatic as ever. But the main impression left by this last volume is of the author wrestling, as Trotsky himself wrestled, with the profoundest problems of the Russian revolution and its destiny – its victories and its defeats, its achievements and its crimes. Mr Deutscher is to be congratulated on having brought a great enterprise to a worthy conclusion.

X *Unfinished Revolution*

THE October revolution of 1917 may reasonably be celebrated on its fiftieth anniversary as the greatest event of the twentieth century. It is unlikely to occupy a less conspicuous place in the history of the future than the French revolution, of which it was in some respects the sequel and the culmination. If we reflect on the state of the historiography of the French revolution fifty years after the event (Carlyle's *French Revolution*, the first imaginative attempt to treat it as a great historical phenomenon, appeared in 1837), we may be less discouraged by the evident shortcomings of contemporary historical writing about the Russian revolution. Where so much – and so much evil as well as so much good – has flowed directly or indirectly from an outstanding historical event, and where so many interests have been shattered and so many passions aroused by it, half a century is a short span of time in which to place it in a just perspective.

The selection of Mr Isaac Deutscher to deliver the Trevelyan lectures for 1967 in Cambridge was clearly an invitation to celebrate the jubilee year (which is incidentally also the centenary of the first volume of *Das Kapital*) by a review of the achievements and significance of the revolution. Mr Deutscher responded nobly in the lectures now published under the title *The Unfinished Revolution*.[1] Readers familiar with his biographies of Stalin and Trotsky will not need to be reminded of the vividness and energy of his style; the argument is deployed in the narrow compass of this brief survey with the same drive and conviction

[1] I. Deutscher, *The Unfinished Revolution. Russia 1917–1967* (1967).

as in his larger works. Readers will also recognize the same blend of faith in the ultimate destiny of the revolution with an essential humanity of outlook. Mr Deutscher's Marxist background allows him to retain an optimism and a belief in progress more characteristic, in the western world, of the nineteenth century than of the present age. How important this is for the historian of the Russian revolution may be judged by measuring the distance between the dull and grudging belittlement of its achievements in many current western accounts and Mr Deutscher's sympathetic, though also profoundly critical, understanding.

The starting-point must be a recognition of the magnitude of the task confronting the Bolsheviks who seized power in Petrograd fifty years ago. It has recently become fashionable to stress the beginnings of industrialization in the Russia of the 1890s under Witte, with the implication that Russia had already begun to industrialize herself before 1914, and that all that the revolution did was to continue – and perhaps temporarily to delay – the process. This is from more than one point of view an unhistorical fantasy. Witte lost the Tsar's favour – and his office – in 1903, and by 1914 much of the steam had gone out of his policies. The hostility of the land-owning interest which had brought about Witte's downfall would have been fatal to any far-reaching development of industry. This could have occurred only at the expense of their way of life and of the quasi-feudal society which they represented; it was only after their overthrow by the revolution that the modernization of the Russian economy could be undertaken. The industrialization of the 1890s provided a valuable foundation – notably a vital, though limited, network of railways and an embryonic heavy industry – on which later work could be built. It hastened the revolution – perhaps even made it possible – by bringing into existence a small, but concentrated, factory proletariat. But it lacked the fundamental drive which the revolution afterwards imparted to the process.

In another respect, also, the industrialization carried out by the Bolsheviks differed profoundly from the work initiated by Witte. Mr Deutscher quotes the percentages of foreign capital invested in some of Russia's leading industries before 1914: 'Western shareholders owned 90 per cent of Russia's mines, 50 per cent of her chemical industry, over 40 per cent of her engineering plants, and 42 per cent of her banking stock.' Just as the Indian economy has suffered in the past twenty years from distortions created by the legacy of past British investment, so the shape of Russian industry was moulded by the foreign investor who furnished the capital; in this case, the motive of the distortion was mainly military. Mr Deutscher remarks that it was Russia's dependence on foreign capital which compelled the Provisional Government of 1917 to stay in the war, and thus hastened the Bolshevik revolution. This may be an exaggeration. But it is clearly true that the withholding of foreign capital after the revolution, though it was the source of enormous hardships and difficulties, was a powerful influence in shaping the lines which the process of industrialization eventually took; and, in spite of its immense human and material cost, it is difficult to see any other course which could so rapidly have raised Russia, and the Russian people, to their present levels of industrial achievement and material welfare.

It is indeed difficult to do justice to the magnitude and the astonishing speed of this process – starting in a country devastated by seven years of war and civil war, and interrupted by a further and still more destructive war. The major symptom of what has been gained is what Mr Deutscher calls 'the massive urbanization of the USSR'. An increase in the urban population of 100 millions since 1917 means that town-dwellers, who formed 15 per cent of the population before the revolution, now account for nearly 60 per cent. The mass migration from countryside to town, the transformation of the peasant into a factory or office worker, which has been the main factor in bringing about this change, has been, of course, only one element in a more comprehensive process. Literacy has come to the whole population, including the non-Russian peoples of the outlying regions of European Russia and of Central Asia. Education is within the reach of all, and higher education of many. Men and women whose fathers and grandfathers were peasants, and whose great-grandfathers were serfs, operate, design and invent the most sophisticated modern machines. In the space of fifty years a primitive and backward people has been enabled to build up for itself a new kind of life and a new civilization. The magnitude, the extent and the speed of this advance are surely without parallel.

It would be wrong to pass over in silence – and Mr Deutscher is not tempted to do so – the cost of this operation in human suffering, or its other ambiguous aspects. The most cruel burdens fell on the peasants who formed the mass of the Russian people. The drawing off of surplus population from the land, the reorganization of agriculture and the introduction of modern and large-scale methods of cultivation were a necessity if the country was to move forward and take its place in the modern world. The callousness and the brutalities with which the task was accomplished can be explained by the conditions in which it was undertaken – notably by the weakness of the regime in the countryside and the alienation of the peasant from it – but have left their stain on subsequent Soviet history. The spread of knowledge, enlightenment and scientific sophistication, real and immensely significant though it has been, has taken place within a rigidly confined ideological framework, and to the accompaniment of a relentless persecution of heretical opinions; and, though similar symptoms have been present in some of the great intellectual movements of the past in the western world, the degree of intellectual regimentation in the Soviet Union – thanks in part to the scope and suddenness of the explosion, and in part to modern technical facilities – has been extraordinarily rigid and severe. The ambiguities of de-Stalinization have thrown the underlying struggle into sharp relief. It is significant, and perhaps encouraging, that the controversy about the necessary and permissible degree of intellectual freedom is today being carried on with a hitherto unusual frankness and publicity in Soviet journals.

Mr Deutscher approaches tentatively and with some misgivings the problem of the new groups of bureaucrats, technocrats, managers and top-ranking intellectuals, who have been popularized in some recent writings as a 'new class' – a class living, in the Marxist sense, on the surplus value produced by the worker and constituting an exploiting class. The existence of these materially privileged strata in Soviet society is open and apparent. On the other hand, it does not seem that they are sufficiently homogeneous to have developed the close bonds of common interest and common outlook which are the essential basis of a 'class', or that they have either the will or the capacity to act as a united pressure group in Soviet politics. Mr Deutscher derives their peculiar quality, as a class and yet not a class, from two specific features. They enjoy privileges exclusively in respect of consumption and not of accumulation: they cannot acquire property in the means of production, and become capitalists or members of a bourgeoisie in the Marxist sense. And it follows from this that the group does not and cannot consolidate itself. It has no inherited property, and is dissolved and re-formed from one generation to the next. As long as Soviet society retains its fluidity, it will remain revolutionary.

The same answer applies in part to the problem of equality in modern industrial society. Marx, who analysed the contemporary world through deeply absorbed Hegelian categories of thought, believed that what he called 'abstract human labour' had been perverted by the division of labour, which was the characteristic tool of capitalism, into an object of exploitation. The division of labour was a fundamental evil; and it was only when this was overcome that the worker would emerge no longer as an object, but as an individual in his own right. This would in turn involve the disappearance of the distinction not only between the urban and the rural worker (the peasant was already a dying class under capitalism), but also between mental and physical labour, between brain and brawn. These conceptions were rooted in Marxist thinking, and found their expression in Lenin's vision, in *State and Revolution*, of the now simplified tasks of administration performed by ordinary workers in rotation, and in early experiments, after the victory of the revolution, in workers' control over the factories.

Marx seems to have remained convinced that industrial and technological development would lead to a greater uniformity and not to a further diversification of labour; and a certain tendency can undoubtedly be found in modern conditions to efface or blur the line of demarcation between skilled and unskilled labour. But the main development in the most advanced modern industries has been to call for the creation of a large elite of managers, scientists and skilled technicians, far removed from the mass of relatively unskilled and unspecialized workers who will in any foreseeable future remain a numerical majority in the labour force. Lenin did not shrink from preaching the necessity for a political elite when he came to consider the organization and functioning of the party; and after the revolution he found himself making eloquent pleas for 'one-man management' in the factory. In the 1930s Stalin imparted his usual element of cynicism into his denunciation of 'levelling' as a bourgeois prejudice. But he had put his finger on a real problem, and one by no means confined to the Soviet Union.

Revolutions do not easily live down the utopian visions which have inspired them. Indeed it may be said that a society which has no Utopia to revisit is in a state of decay. But to peer into the future is, as Marx knew, a hazardous job; and it is easier to analyse the direction than to postulate the goal. Mr Deutscher has his Utopias for the Russian revolution. When he contemplates the Utopia of Liberty, he is content to build it out of the bricks of the past. The Soviet Union, whose revolution contained bourgeois as well as proletarian elements, has still to catch up with the old 'bourgeois liberal programmes': 'It needs to obtain control over its governments and to transform the state . . . into an instrument of the nation's democratically expressed will and interest. It needs, in the first instance, to re-establish freedom of expression and association.' But the Utopia of Equality, of the classless and stateless society, is more intangible, and more difficult to define or describe. Mr Deutscher ends his chapter on the social structure of the USSR with the reflection that the spread of secondary education is creating an intelligentsia in larger numbers than can be absorbed by the universities and in non-manual occupations, and that the consequent growth of an educated stratum of the working class will press heavily on the bureaucratic and managerial strata above. It may be that these pressures will result in enforcing a greater equality of status between manual and non-manual workers, such as has occurred in some western countries. No advanced society is likely in any future that can be foreseen to renounce in principle the ideal of equality. But a large mark of interrogation hangs over the question how equality is to be realized – or even defined – in modern industrial society.

The relations of the USSR to the outside world is a topic of absorbing interest which has naturally attracted more attention abroad than any other aspect of Soviet policy. Here Mr Deutscher presents, no doubt for reasons of space, a rather simplified picture. He begins by pointing out that all orthodox Marxists, including the early Bolshevik leaders, looked forward to the socialist revolution as an international event, and effectively quotes Engels's denunciation of the narrow-mindedness of socialists who believed that their own nation was destined by its own efforts to achieve the victory of socialism. Belief in the international character of the revolution was firmly held and inculcated by Lenin down to the time of his death.

Then, in the middle 1920s, Stalin and Bukharin, with Trotsky, Kamenev and Zinoviev in opposition, propounded the famous doctrine of socialism in one country. This led to the identification of the interests of socialism with Russian national interest. In the pursuit of national security, Stalin soft-pedalled the cause of the socialist revolution elsewhere, muzzled and eventually dissolved the Comintern, and did his misguided best to insulate his country from involvement in foreign conflicts. Hence the refusal to allow German communists to collaborate with the Social-Democratic Party in resisting the rise of Hitler; hence the Soviet-German pact of 1939, the acceptance in 1945 of the partition of Europe into zones of influence, and the failure to support the Chinese communists against Chiang Kai-shek down to the very moment when they proved victorious by their own exertions. All these were disastrous instances of the subordination of the interests of socialism and world revolution to a narrowly conceived *Realpolitik*. It is not surprising that the socialists of other countries have by and large turned against the USSR.

The picture is correct so far as it goes. But it perhaps fails to do justice to a dilemma which the makers of Soviet foreign policy have faced from the beginning, and still face today. Lenin, at the time of Brest-Litovsk, had to meet a charge from his more idealistic followers of sacrificing the true socialist cause by seeking an accommodation with an imperialist power, and defended himself on the ground of the need to preserve the socialist revolution in the one country where it had been achieved. In the trade agreement with Great Britain in 1921, and at the Genoa conference in the following year, Lenin showed himself willing to seek peaceful coexistence with the western powers through an implied or explicit promise to call off Soviet propaganda for world revolution. It is true that, where Lenin had merely leaned a little to one side of the fence, Stalin came down with a bump. But the fence was there, and it was impossible to sit on it indefinitely. Stalin might have argued that Lenin had at least pointed in that direction.

The story of the 1930s is inevitably told nowadays with the hindsight of 1939 and after. Mr Deutscher notes with some apparent surprise that, in spite of de-Stalinization, the Soviet-German pact has never been held up to opprobrium. The reason seems clear. Nothing could be easier than to condemn Stalin for concluding the pact. But on what grounds would the condemnation rest? Was Stalin wrong to come to terms with Hitler because he chose the wrong side? Or was he wrong to come to terms with any imperialist power? In other words, would the condemnation extend to the Litvinov policy of the middle 1930s – the entry into the League of Nations, the endorsement of the Versailles treaty, the Franco-Soviet pact and the instruction to communists of western Europe to operate united front policies? Mr Deutscher does not make his position quite clear. But a derogatory passing reference to the Popular Front in France seems to imply that he would be critical of all these policies.

This indeed is the only position consistent with unqualified belief in an international socialism ultimately overriding national interests; and this is, of course, the basis of the anathemas which Mao Tse-tung hurls today at the Soviet leaders. But can the Soviet leaders even today escape the dilemma which confronted Lenin of defending the socialist revolution in their own country? No doubt voices are heard at this moment in the inner councils of Moscow wondering whether it was really necessary for Mr Kosygin to sit in amicable conference with President Johnson, the arch-capitalist, when he might have been devoting all his energies to the promotion of the revolutionary cause in the Far or Middle East. But is this a realistic assessment? There is every sign that Mr Kosygin is doing his best to return to the fence-sitting position adopted by Lenin in the early 1920s – a position familiar to diplomats and to politicians of all complexions, though not perhaps easy to reconcile with a rigid adherence to revolutionary principles.

The penultimate chapter of Mr Deutscher's work is devoted to an illuminating analysis of Soviet-Chinese relations in which he shows Mao Tse-tung also straddling the policies of international socialism and of national self-sufficiency, and convicts him of having followed in Indonesia the misguided Stalinist line of restraining the local communists in the supposed interests of friendship with the Sukarno regime, and with the same disastrous results. In the last chapter he reverts to the significance of the Russian revolution for the western world. He will have no truck with the theory of the gradual and almost unperceived growing of our modern capitalist economies into socialism.

The fact is that, regardless of all Keynesian innovations, our productive process, so magnificently socialized in many respects, is not yet socially controlled . . . the test is whether our society can control and marshal its resources and energies for constructive purposes and for its own general welfare. . . . Until now our society has failed this test. Our governments have forestalled slumps and depressions by planning for destruction and death rather than for life and welfare.

Little consolation can be found in the prospect of a 'stalemate indefinitely prolonged, and guaranteed by a perpetual balance of nuclear deterrents'. The stupendous progress made by backward Russia over the past fifty years in face of the most adverse conditions points the way to what the western nations might achieve by giving effect to 'the great principle of a new social organization'. With this eloquent and well argued appeal Mr Deutscher ends what is in every way a remarkable and masterly book.

Isaac Deutscher:
In Memoriam

THE sudden and premature death of Isaac Deutscher on 19 August 1967 at the age of sixty was a tragic blow to scholarship. Coming less than six months after he had completed his memorable Trevelyan Lectures on *Fifty Years of the Russian Revolution*, it will have made a particularly painful impact on many members of this University, where the size and enthusiasm of his audience in the Mill Lane lecture rooms, largely composed of undergraduates, are still recalled. The lectures were solid fare, and owed their wide appeal not to any element of fireworks or sensationalism, but to their patient and searching analysis of events whose immense significance for the contemporary world is apparent to all, but which find little place in our current university teaching. Nobody who listened to the lectures could doubt either the range and depth of Isaac Deutscher's learning or the balance and humanity of his judgements. His approach to his subject was both acutely critical and profoundly sympathetic, as far removed from the spirit of official eulogy and white-washing as from the spirit of carping hostility still characteristic of some western writing about the revolution. The lectures, published in June 1967 under the title *The Unfinished Revolution*, were his last work.

Deutscher was a convinced and committed Marxist. He came to Marxism very early in life by way of reaction from a Jewish rabbinical background. An admirer of Lenin, he was never in the remotest degree a Stalinist. He was a follower of Trotsky only in the formal sense that he broke with the Polish Communist Party in his middle twenties on the issue of the intolerant and brutal treatment meted out to Trotsky by Stalin and the party majority; as readers of his biography of Trotsky know, his admiration for his hero was tempered by criticisms and qualifications on many vital points. Deutscher had his roots both in Marxism and, like Marx himself, in the humanism of the Enlightenment. He derived from both these sources a belief in progress and an optimism about the future destinies of the human race which would not have seemed singular in nineteenth-century England, but which sometimes exposed him to derisory comment in the more cynical and guilt-laden western world of today. No charge was more frequently made against his journalistic writings than that of an excessive optimism.

The works by which his name will live are his one-volume biography of Stalin published in 1949 and his three-volume biography of Trotsky published between 1954 and 1963. The latter must surely rank as the outstanding historical biography of our time. The approach to history through biography sometimes seems an easy option, and more often than not proves unrewarding. But Deutscher's Marxism gave him a profound and continuous consciousness of the historical process, and saved him from any temptation to reduce it to a study of the psychological idiosyncrasies of the actors. When Deutscher wrote biography, his theme was history seen through the actions of individuals. His two major biographies afford vivid and unforgettable portraits of Stalin and, more especially, of Trotsky. But they are also a part – and indeed a large part – of the history of the Russian revolution; and it is a matter of pride and satisfaction that this university should have provided him, a few months before his life was tragically cut short, with the occasion and the platform to present his balance-sheet of the achievements of the revolution – of its grandeurs and of its miseries. *The Unfinished Revolution* will stand with the two biographies as a great monument to his name. It is sad to think that, in a field of history where both scholarship and balanced judgement are in short supply, we have been deprived at so early an age of a scholar so exceptionally equipped with both.

A Note About the Author

E. H. Carr was born in London in 1892 and educated at Trinity College, Cambridge. He was attached to the British delegation at the Peace Conference in 1919 and was a member of the department dealing with Russian affairs in the British Foreign Office following the Bolshevik Revolution. He resigned from the Foreign Office in 1936 to become Professor of International Politics at the University College of Wales. From 1941 to 1946 he was an assistant editor of *The Times* of London and from 1953 to 1955 a tutor in Politics, Balliol College, Oxford. Since 1955 he has been a fellow of Trinity College, Cambridge. He is the author of many books in addition to *What is History?* and his multivolumed *A History of Soviet Russia*.